KNOCKALOE
INTERNMENT CAMP
100 YEARS OF HISTORY

Rosalind Stimpson with Stephen Hall

Translations by Laura M. Wenzlaw
and Sarah Brandstätter

Lily Publications

www.lilypublications.co.uk

KNOCKALOE INTERNMENT CAMP

Christmas 1917. Art card by F. Nettal with great attention to detail: notice the moon-lit barbed wire fences through the window.

Front cover: A very atmospheric art card showing the camp at night.
Back cover: There were printing presses in the camp and and some very skilled work was done as illustrated by this steel engraving of the camp.

Published by:
Lily Publications (IOM) Ltd,
PO Box 33, Ramsey, Isle of Man IM99 4LP
Tel: +44 (0) 1624 898446
Fax: +44 (0) 1624 898449
E-mail: info@lilypublications.co.uk
www.lilypublications.co.uk

Copyright © 2014 Lily Publications. All rights reserved. Reprinted 2022.

ISBN 978-1-911177-88-3

The right of Rosalind Stimpson to be identified as the author of this work has been asserted in accordance with the Copyright Act 1991. Images © Stephen Hall unless noted otherwise. No part of this publication may be reproduced, stored in a retrieval system or transmitted in any form or by any means, electronic, mechanical, photocopying, recording or otherwise, without prior permission in writing from the publisher.

Knockaloe Camp 1914-1919

A month after the outbreak of the First World War, the British Government utilised the new Aliens Restriction Act, interning enemy aliens on the Isle of Man. The first camp for which was in Douglas.

In the autumn of 1914, a deputation from the Civilian Internment Camps Committee visited the Isle of Man with the task of discovering a location suitable for a second Internment Camp on the Island. Sir William Byrne, Mr. Edmund Montefiore, with Dr. C. H. Bond of the Board of Control, as medical advisor, visited the Island on the 24th October.

According to the *Ramsey Courier,* dated 30th October 1914, the gentlemen held conference with Manx Government officials discussing the possibility of a camp that could hold a number of Civilian Interns that surpassed that of the current Douglas Camp, as there were various reports of malcontent. The interns were not to be "belligerents actually captured in battle" however, but for "several classes of alien enemies who may require concentration". This included "the suspect, dangerous or belligerent class, who may require strictly military camp, with close custody and guard" in addition to "women and children and elderly men, who, for the most part, are in no sense a danger to this country". British

1915 watercolour painting showing one of the more picturesque views of the Knockaloe camp with the hills in the background. This viewpoint can be seen in a number of other works.

women married to German nationals and their British children were considered legal aliens, though not necessarily a threat. They were accommodated in boarding houses throughout the Island while visiting the men.

Only a day later than this report, on the 31st October, the *Isle of Man Examiner* contained a recruitment advertisement: "WANTED, at once, about 30 JOINERS, —Apply, Detention Camp, Knockaloe, Near Peel." Knockaloe had been the clear choice for the site, having previously been used as a Territorial troops camping ground. The first prisoners were to arrive less than a fortnight later, on the 12th November. Only five days later, a riot erupted in the Douglas Camp, resulting in the deaths of five internees. From this it is clear that, contrary to general belief, the riot was not the reason Knockaloe Camp was initially constructed.

Originally built to accommodate 5,000 aliens and a guard of at least 500 in 1914, then an additional 5,000 interns in May 1915 (and further additions as the war continued), Knockaloe Camp eventually grew to a size holding approximately 23,000 internees. With a circumference of three miles, the camp was split into 23 compounds of 1,000 men; wooden huts covered 22 acres and were divided between four camps. Each camp had its own hospital, theatre and kitchen among other necessities. The camp had its

Art card by G. Stoltz showing several scenes of the camp. Notice the Manx cat and shield with Manx triskellion superimposed on the map of the Island. Note also the traditional Manx thatched cottage with guard's hut in the bottom left.

own power station to provide the lighting for 7,156 bulbs and 72 miles of electric cable.

The camp's 170 tons of barbed-wire fencing, 15 million feet of timber, and 900 thousand bricks incorporated in the buildings were all dismantled the year following the end of the First World War, in 1919. The camp's Quartermaster, Mr. J. H. Cubbon, remained in employment at the camp from its formation to its dismantling and over the course of the war logged the following:

> 145,000 socks
> 125,000 blankets
> 100,000 towels
> 80,000 shirts
> 90,000 clogs
> 593 tons of soap
> 204 miles of flannel
> 113 miles of Moleskin

Receipt dated November 1914 from John Kermode (whose shop exterior looks the same today) for 55 bales of blankets containing 4,000 blankets and 55 wrappers.

The vast amounts of supplies were brought to the camp via a special branch railway line. In 1915, an extension of the line serving Peel was built along the quay wall and up towards the camp. The engine *Caledonia* served various parts of the camp including the laundry, the hospital, the Quartermaster's stores and the bakery. The bakery is particularly noteworthy as, for the camp of 26,000 (including staff, troops and interns), many prisoners were employed within the bakery and 15,000 two-pound loaves were baked daily when the camp was full.

Despite the large quantity of essentials being brought into the camp, Knockaloe did not contain a Privilege Camp, unlike Douglas, where interns could pay for private rooms and purchase more home comforts. A great deal of food and clothing and other such necessities were made by the interns themselves. Members of the Jewish communities were, however, given facilities to celebrate Jewish festivals and provided with kosher food.

The interns made the most of their internment, as far as they were able. School facilities were provided and education encouraged, particularly for younger interns. Craftwork filled hours of many interns' days, from bone or wood carving to wicker-basket making. Many interns also joined theatre or music groups, performing concerts or plays for their fellows.

Many interns also worked for a small wage, specifically on nearby farmland. Interns were hired out to farmers and were employed by the government in groups of up to 100 men. This was in order to reclaim waste land assigned to the government by farmers for the

Picture postcard of a teacher training college set up within the camp. Inmates went to enormous lengths to organise activities to educate and keep themselves busy and productive. This card was sent by Reinhard Gotterg P.O.W. 9727 camp II compound 4 hut b, on 16th January 1918.

duration of the war. Several other schemes were introduced for the useful employment of the prisoners. Quarrying and road making for the highway board were carried by interns in groups of 50 men, and work camps were formed at Regaby, Ramsey and Ballaugh to provide farmers with extra labour. The Sulby River was widened and deepened by prisoners for a considerable part of its course, and peat on the mountain was also cut back by interns. A great deal of flat-pack furniture was also built in the camp to send to parts of Europe that has been heavily bombed and where families were without basics such as chairs and tables.

Sport was a welcome distraction from the barbed-wire fences and tiresome captivity, as many teams of varying sports were played. Several sports days and competition programmes still exist and record the events that lessened the monotony of Civilian Internment.

Many art cards and postcards were also designed by the interns and it is these original designs that have survived, marked on the reverse with messages home to loved ones. A great deal of the designs are said to be inspired by Manx artist Archibald Knox who, along with Mr W. M. Holmes, was in charge of the censorship of mail at the camp. Censoring the mail was an arduous job, and Knox, as well as others, would have had to be most painstaking in order to ensure that seditious messages did not evade them. B.E. Sargeaunt, Government Secretary and Treasurer to the Isle of Man during the period, noted that even walnuts would have to be opened in case a message had been concealed inside.

Knockaloe Camp remained open after the Armistice until the autumn of 1919; this was simply because it took almost a year to send the then 24,450 interns home. Only sixteen per cent of these were permitted to take up residence again in Britain. The last 175 prisoners were marched out of the camp in October 1919, and escorted to peel en route to freedom.

Most of the furniture, wood and even barbed wire that made up the camp was dismantled and sold throughout the Island and elsewhere. Little physical evidence now remains in the fields of Knockaloe Farm that such an important segment of the Isle of Man's war effort took place there. Its legacy still lives on, though, through the research and collections of enthusiasts worldwide.

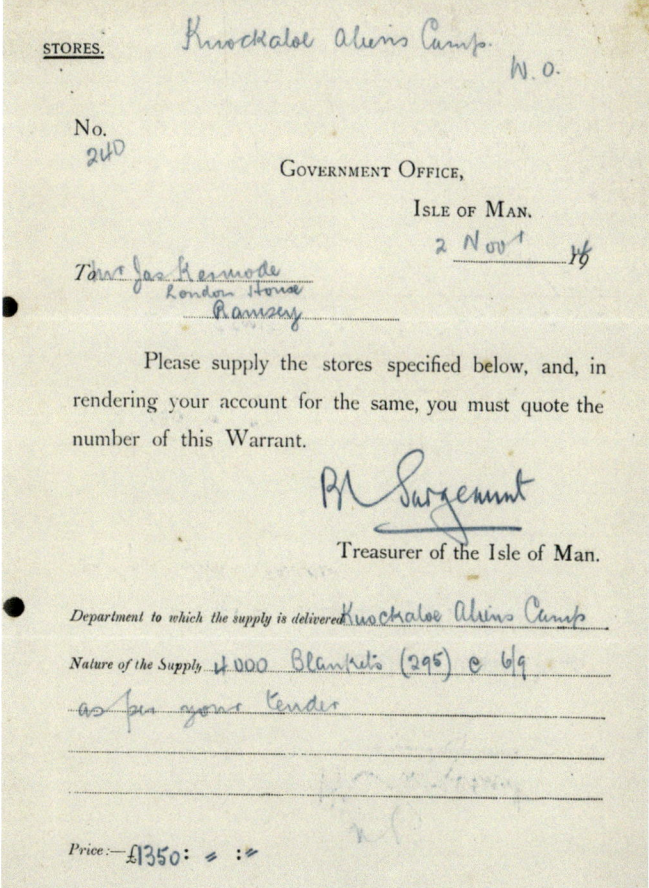

Government order to John Kermode requesting supplies for Knockaloe and signed for by B.E. Sergeaunt who was Treasurer of the Isle of Man.

Stephen Hall

Stephen Hall is a Supervisor working at the Manx Electric Railway in Douglas on the Isle of Man.

Stephen began collecting Knockaloe Camp relics in 2004, after buying art cards from friend Les Clarke in Ramsey on the Isle of Man. Having had little knowledge of the camp and its importance during the First World War, Stephen decided to visit the site himself. The discovery of the history behind the few beautifully designed cards began a search for other items linked to the camp which was so important to the Island during the war.

Scouring auctions in Europe and online, Stephen now has a vast collection of art cards, postcards, letters, trinkets, receipts, carvings and much more, all of which relate to or were made in Knockaloe Camp. Aware that this stunning and extensive collection is of such importance to understanding the way of life within the camp, Stephen has decided to share a selection of his favourite pieces.

A great deal of his collection has been returned to the Island from Germany, much of which contains letters and cards to and from internees about whom little is known. Stephen is anxious to discover as much

KNOCKALOE INTERNMENT CAMP

These beautiful pen and ink drawings illustrate various aspects of a day in camp life through the eyes of the artist P.O.W. Behrens, in camp III. Close observation will show that the prisoners had holes in their sock and underwear, took part in gymnastics, painted, kept rabbits, played music and watched staged performances amongst other things.

as possible about the people who spent so long inside the camp without knowing their release date, and reveals much of his collection in the hope that these small segments of the interns' lives may be recognised and thereby his questions concerning them answered.

In July 2014, Stephen assisted at a dig run by the Centre for Manx Studies, University of Liverpool Department of Archaeology at the site of the camp, Knockaloe Farm, in Patrick. The team were able to unearth tell-tale signs of the interns' presence so many years ago, such as assorted pottery and glass fragments, including the remains of an inkwell, as well as some well-worn shoes. These were in addition to remains of the camp's water and sewerage systems, including metal and ceramic pipes. The team also discovered the camp's outer boundaries, with the remnants of the corner concrete post-holes which held the original fence in place.

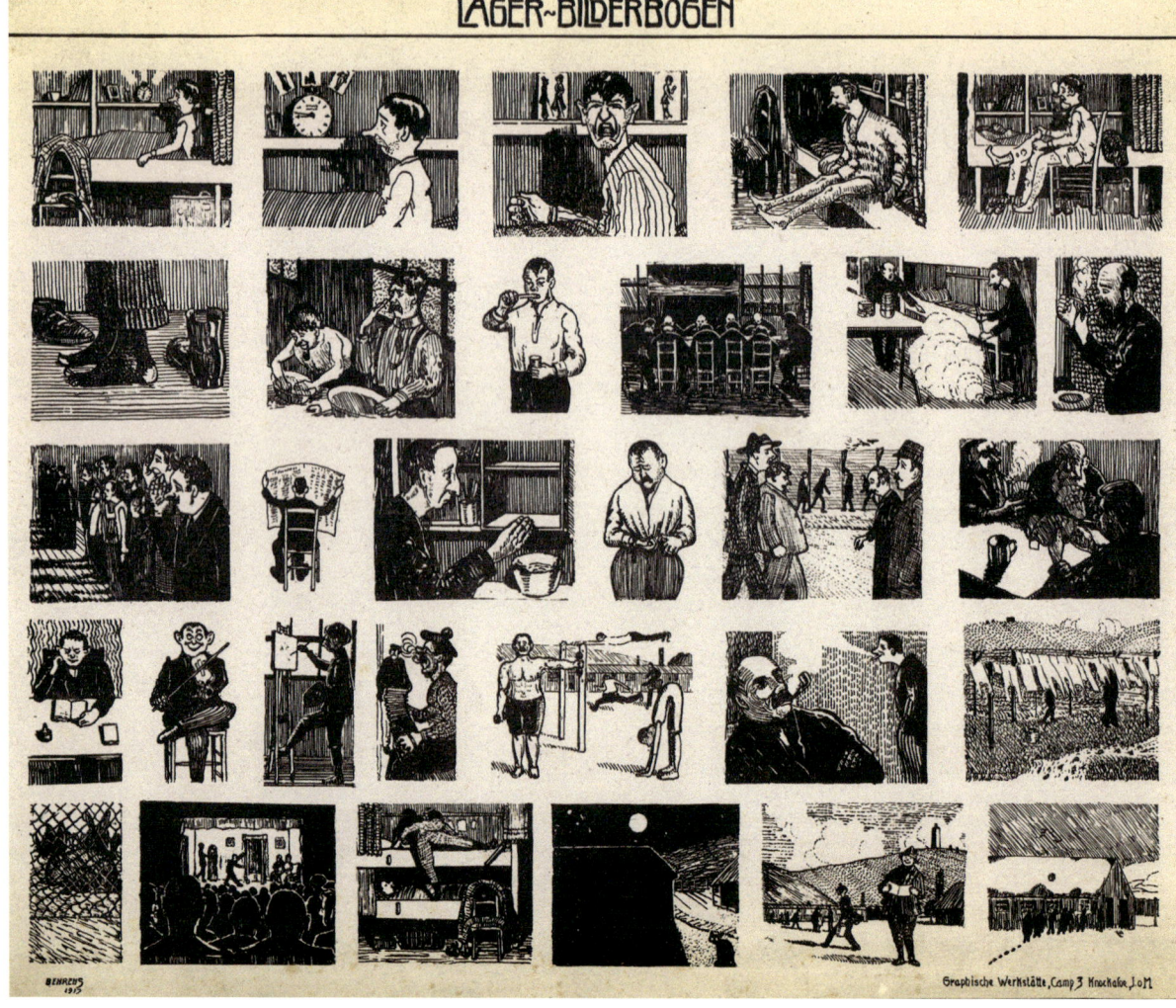

100 YEARS OF HISTORY

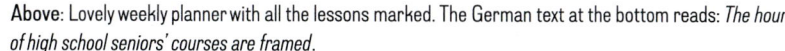

Bibliography

Boyd, James I.C., *The Isle of Man Railway*, (published 1962 by The Oakwood Press, Surrey).

Cresswell, Yvonne M. (ed.), *Living with the Wire: Civilian Internment in the Isle of Man during the two World Wars*, (published 2010 by Manx National Heritage, The Manx Museum, Douglas).

Isle of Man Examiner (31st October 1914, p.4).

Ling, Peter and Joy, *For King and Country: Ballaugh in the Great War— 1914-1918*, (printed 2014 by The Copy Shop, Douglas).

Ramsey Courier (30th October 1914, p.4 and 6).

Sargeaunt, B.E., *The Isle of Man and the Great War*, (published 1920 by Brown and Sons Ltd., Douglas).

Above: Lovely weekly planner with all the lessons marked. The German text at the bottom reads: *The hours of high school seniors' courses are framed*.
Right: Picture postcard of first aider, sent from P.O.W. Erinering, posted 1st November 1916.

Two real picture postcards.
Above: Boxers from the camp athletics team in 1915.

Right: Camp theatre in more ways than one as this group of smiling detainees dressed as women.

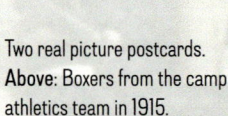

Above: One of the camp orchestras. Many internees were trained and very competent musicians and music seemed to be an important part of camp life.

Left: Colour postcard depicting the camp surrounded by a decorative barbed wire border. This is an excellent representation of what the huts looked like. These cards were probably printed in black and white and colour tinted later by hand.

KNOCKALOE INTERNMENT CAMP

A picture postcard depicting a guard in one of the camp canteens. The products of messrs Cadbury are prominent and boxes of Oxo can be seen on the shelves behind.

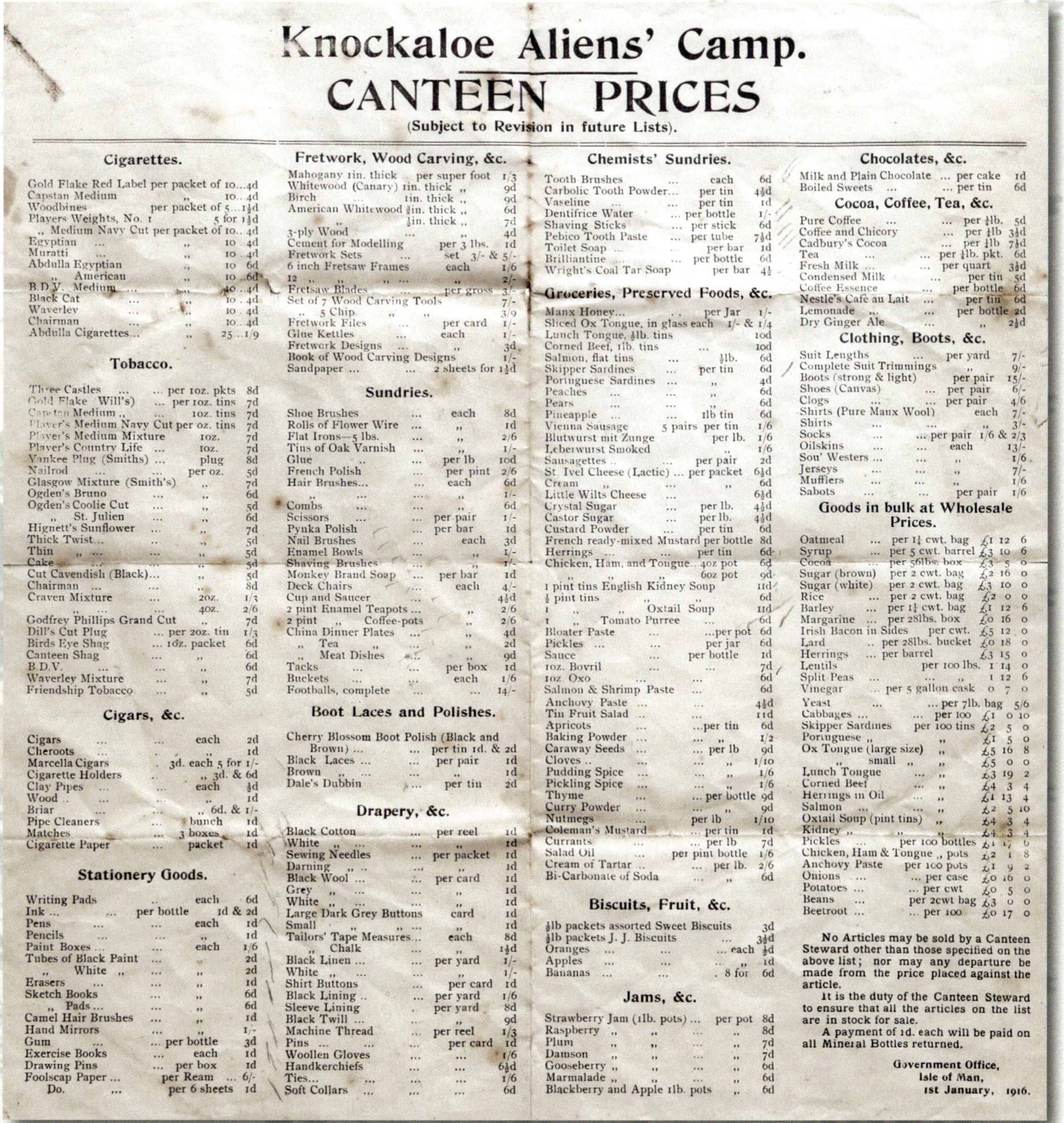

Knockaloe Aliens' Camp.

CANTEEN PRICES

(Subject to Revision in future Lists).

Cigarettes.

Gold Flake Red Label	per packet of 10	4d
Capstan Medium	,, 10	4d
Woodbines	per packet of 5	1½d
Players Weights, No. 1	5 for	1½d
,, Medium Navy Cut	per packet of 10	4d
Egyptian	,, 10	4d
Muratti	,, 10	4d
Abdulla Egyptian	,, 10	6d
,, American	,, 10	6d
B.D.V. Medium	,, 10	4d
Black Cat	,, 10	4d
Waverley	,, 10	4d
Chairman	,, 10	4d
Abdulla Cigarettes	,, 25	1/9

Tobacco.

Three Castles	per 1oz. pkts	8d
Gold Flake (Will's)	per 1oz. tins	7d
Capstan Medium ,,	1oz. tins	7d
Player's Medium Navy Cut	per oz. tins	7d
Player's Medium Mixture	1oz.	7d
Player's Country Life	1oz.	7d
Yankee Plug (Smiths)	plug	8d
Nailrod	per oz.	5d
Glasgow Mixture (Smith's)	,,	7d
Ogden's Bruno	,,	6d
Ogden's Coolie Cut	,,	5d
,, St. Julien	,,	6d
Hignett's Sunflower	,,	7d
Thick Twist	,,	5d
Thin ,,	,,	5d
Cake	,,	5d
Cut Cavendish (Black)	,,	5d
Chairman	,,	8d
Craven Mixture	2oz.	1/3
,,	4oz.	2/6
Godfrey Phillips Grand Cut	,,	7d
Dill's Cut Plug	per 2oz. tin	1/3
Birds Eye Shag	1oz. packet	6d
Canteen Shag	,,	6d
B.D.V.	,,	6d
Waverley Mixture	,,	7d
Friendship Tobacco	,,	5d

Cigars, &c.

Cigars	each	2d
Cheroots	,,	1d
Marcella Cigars	3d. each 5 for	1/-
Cigarette Holders	,, 3d. &	6d
Clay Pipes	each	½d
Wood	,,	1d
Briar	,, 6d. &	1/-
Pipe Cleaners	bunch	1d
Matches	3 boxes	1d
Cigarette Paper	packet	1d

Stationery Goods.

Writing Pads	each	6d
Ink	per bottle	1d & 2d
Pens	each	1d
Pencils	,,	1d
Paint Boxes	each	1/6
Tubes of Black Paint	,,	2d
,, White ,,	,,	2d
Erasers	,,	1d
Sketch Books	,,	6d
,, Pads	,,	6d
Camel Hair Brushes	,,	1d
Hand Mirrors	,,	1/-
Gum	per bottle	3d
Exercise Books	each	1d
Drawing Pins	per box	1d
Foolscap Paper	per Ream	6/-
Do.	per 6 sheets	1d

Fretwork, Wood Carving, &c.

Mahogany 1in. thick	per super foot	1/3
Whitewood (Canary) 1in. thick	,,	9d
Birch 1in. thick	,,	9d
American Whitewood ⅜in. thick	,,	6d
,, ½in. thick	,,	7d
3-ply Wood	,,	4d
Cement for Modelling	per 3 lbs.	1d
Fretwork Sets	set 3/- &	5/-
6 inch Fretsaw Frames	each	1/6
12 ,, ,, ,,	,,	2/-
Fretsaw Blades	per gross	3/-
Set of 7 Wood Carving Tools		7/-
,, 5 Chip ,, ,,		3/9
Fretwork Files	per card	1/-
Glue Kettles	each	1/-
Fretwork Designs	,,	3d
Book of Wood Carving Designs		1/-
Sandpaper	2 sheets for	1½d

Sundries.

Shoe Brushes	each	8d
Rolls of Flower Wire	,,	1d
Flat Irons—5 lbs.	,,	2/6
Tins of Oak Varnish	,,	1/-
Glue	per lb	10d
French Polish	per pint	2/6
Hair Brushes	each	6d
,,	,,	1/-
Combs	,,	6d
Scissors	per pair	1/-
Pynka Polish	per bar	1d
Nail Brushes	each	3d
Enamel Bowls	,,	1/-
Shaving Brushes	,,	1/-
Monkey Brand Soap	per bar	1d
Deck Chairs	each	4/-
Cup and Saucer		4½d
2 pint Enamel Teapots	,,	2/6
2 pint ,, Coffee-pots	,,	2/6
China Dinner Plates	,,	4d
,, Tea ,,	,,	2d
,, Meat Dishes	,,	9d
Tacks	per box	1d
Buckets	each	1/6
Footballs, complete		14/-

Boot Laces and Polishes.

Cherry Blossom Boot Polish (Black and Brown)	per tin 1d. &	2d
Black Laces	per pair	1d
Brown ,,	,,	1d
Dale's Dubbin	per tin	2d

Drapery, &c.

Black Cotton	per reel	1d
White ,,	,,	1d
Sewing Needles	per packet	1d
Darning ,,	,,	1d
Black Wool	per card	1d
Grey ,,	,,	1d
White ,,	,,	1d
Large Dark Grey Buttons	card	1d
Small ,, ,,	,,	1d
Tailors' Tape Measures	each	8d
,, Chalk	,,	1½d
Black Linen	per yard	1/-
White ,,	,,	1/-
Shirt Buttons	per card	1d
Black Lining	per yard	1/6
Sleeve Lining	per yard	8d
Black Twill	,,	9d
Machine Thread	per reel	1/3
Pins	per card	1d
Woollen Gloves		1/6
Handkerchiefs		6½d
Ties		1/6
Soft Collars		6d

Chemists' Sundries.

Tooth Brushes	each	6d
Carbolic Tooth Powder	per tin	4½d
Vaseline	per tin	1d
Dentifrice Water	per bottle	1/-
Shaving Sticks	per stick	6d
Pebico Tooth Paste	per tube	7½d
Toilet Soap	per bar	1d
Brilliantine	per bottle	6d
Wright's Coal Tar Soap	per bar	4½

Groceries, Preserved Foods, &c.

Manx Honey	per Jar	1/-
Sliced Ox Tongue, in glass	each 1/- &	1/4
Lunch Tongue, ½lb. tins		10d
Corned Beef, 1lb. tins		10d
Salmon, flat tins	½lb.	6d
Skipper Sardines	per tin	6d
Portuguese Sardines	,,	4d
Peaches	,,	6d
Pears	,,	6d
Pineapple	1lb tin	6d
Vienna Sausage	5 pairs per tin	1/6
Blutwurst mit Zunge	per lb.	1/6
Leberwurst Smoked	,,	1/6
Sausagettes	per pair	2d
St. Ivel Cheese (Lactic)	per packet	6½d
Cream ,,	,,	6d
Little Wilts Cheese		6½d
Crystal Sugar	per lb.	4½d
Castor Sugar	per lb.	4½d
Custard Powder	per tin	6d
French ready-mixed Mustard	per bottle	8d
Herrings	per tin	6d
Chicken, Ham, and Tongue	4oz pot	6d
,, ,, ,,	6oz pot	9d
1 pint tins English Kidney Soup		11d
½ pint tins ,, ,,		6d
1 ,, ,, Oxtail Soup		11d
1 ,, Tomato Purree		6d
Bloater Paste	per pot	6d
Pickles	per jar	6d
Sauce	per bottle	1d
1oz. Bovril		7d
1oz. Oxo		6d
Salmon & Shrimp Paste		6d
Anchovy Paste		4½d
Tin Fruit Salad		11d
Apricots	per tin	6d
Baking Powder	,,	1/2
Caraway Seeds	per lb	9d
Cloves	,,	1/10
Pudding Spice	,,	1/6
Pickling Spice	,,	1/6
Thyme	per bottle	9d
Curry Powder	,,	9d
Nutmegs	per lb	1/10
Coleman's Mustard	per tin	1d
Currants	per lb	7d
Salad Oil	per pint bottle	1/6
Cream of Tartar	per lb.	2/6
Bi-Carbonate of Soda	,,	6d

Biscuits, Fruit, &c.

½lb packets assorted Sweet Biscuits		3d
½lb packets J. J. Biscuits		3½d
Oranges	each	½d
Apples	,,	1d
Bananas	8 for	6d

Jams, &c.

Strawberry Jam (1lb. pots)	per pot	8d
Raspberry ,, ,,	,,	8d
Plum ,, ,,	,,	7d
Damson ,, ,,	,,	7d
Gooseberry ,, ,,	,,	6d
Marmalade ,, ,,	,,	6d
Blackberry and Apple 1lb. pots	,,	6d

Chocolates, &c.

Milk and Plain Chocolate	per cake	1d
Boiled Sweets	per tin	6d

Cocoa, Coffee, Tea, &c.

Pure Coffee	per ¼lb.	5d
Coffee and Chicory	per ¼lb	3½d
Cadbury's Cocoa	per ¼lb	7½d
Tea	per ¼lb. pkt.	6d
Fresh Milk	per quart	3½d
Condensed Milk	per tin	5d
Coffee Essence	per bottle	6d
Nestle's Café au Lait	per tin	6d
Lemonade	per bottle	2d
Dry Ginger Ale	,,	2½d

Clothing, Boots, &c.

Suit Lengths	per yard	7/-
Complete Suit Trimmings	,,	9/-
Boots (strong & light)	per pair	15/-
Shoes (Canvas)	per pair	6/-
Clogs	per pair	4/6
Shirts (Pure Manx Wool)	each	7/-
Shirts	,,	3/-
Socks	per pair	1/6 & 2/3
Oilskins	each	13/-
Sou' Westers	,,	1/6
Jerseys	,,	7/-
Mufflers	,,	1/6
Sabots	per pair	1/6

Goods in bulk at Wholesale Prices.

		£	s	d
Oatmeal	per 1¼ cwt. bag	£1	12	6
Syrup	per 5 cwt. barrel	£3	10	6
Cocoa	per 56lbs. box	£3	5	0
Sugar (brown)	per 2 cwt. bag	£2	16	0
Sugar (white)	per 2 cwt. bag	£3	10	0
Rice	per 2 cwt. bag	£2	0	0
Barley	per 1¼ cwt. bag	£1	12	6
Margarine	per 28lbs. box	£0	16	0
Irish Bacon in Sides	per cwt.	£5	12	0
Lard	per 28lbs. bucket	£0	18	0
Herrings	per barrel	£3	15	0
Lentils	per 100 lbs.	1	14	0
Split Peas	,,	1	12	6
Vinegar	per 5 gallon cask	0	7	0
Yeast	per 7lb. bag			5/6
Cabbages	per 100	£1	0	10
Skipper Sardines	per 100 tins	£2	5	0
Portuguese ,,	,,	£1	5	0
Ox Tongue (large size)	,,	£5	16	8
,, small ,,	,,	£5	0	0
Lunch Tongue	,,	£3	19	2
Corned Beef	,,	£4	3	4
Herrings in Oil	,,	£1	13	4
Salmon	,,	£2	5	10
Oxtail Soup (pint tins)	,,	£4	3	4
Kidney ,, ,,	,,	£4	3	4
Pickles	per 100 bottles	£1	17	6
Chicken, Ham & Tongue	,, pots	£2	1	8
Anchovy Paste	per 100 pots	£1	9	2
Onions	per case	£0	16	0
Potatoes	per cwt	£0	5	0
Beans	per 2cwt bag	£3	0	0
Beetroot	per 100	£0	17	0

No Articles may be sold by a Canteen Steward other than those specified on the above list; nor may any departure be made from the price placed against the article.

It is the duty of the Canteen Steward to ensure that all the articles on the list are in stock for sale.

A payment of 1d. each will be paid on all Mineral Bottles returned.

Government Office,
Isle of Man,
1st January, 1916.

Camp canteen price list dated 1st January 1916. This shows what internees in the camp could purchase if they had money – everything from Kidney Soup (not a popular dish these days) to a flat iron to press your clothes with.

KNOCKALOE INTERNMENT CAMP

Letter to B.E. Sargeaunt from John Kermode suppliers as acknowledgment for an order for 3,000 chairs. Pressure from suppliers to try to raise prices was as prevalent then as it is now.

JUNE 4 15.

B.E. SARGEAUNT. Esq.

Dear sir,

I thank you for your esteemed order to hand, Warrant No 32, for 3 000 Chairs for Section No 4, Knockaloe Camp Peel, which I am giving my immediate attention.

Since placing your former order for 6 000 Chairs the makers have written me they have been obliged to advance their prices 10 o/o, owing to the increased cost of Raw material & Labour, (a cutting from one of their letters I enclose), I am however crossing to England on Monday, and shall endeavour to execute your last order at the same price as the former ones, but if I find I am unable to xxux do so I will communicate with you at once, and let you know the very best I can possibly, do.

Thanking you for past favors, and assuring you of my best services.

I am

Yours Faithfully.

Reference No, C/739.

ALIENS' DETENTION CAMP
KNOCKALOE,
ISLE OF MAN.

24th December 1915.

Sir,

I beg to acknowledge receipt of 250 Suits Of Clothing, for which I thank you.

I have the honour to be,

Sir,

Your obedient Servant,

[signature] Lieut,
AND CAMP QUARTERMASTER.

Mr. John Kermode,
    Draper Etc,
        Parliament Street,
            RAMSEY.

A letter to John Kermode as receipt for 250 suits, signed for by the camp quartermaster and dated 24th December 1915 (Christmas Eve). As one of the primary suppliers of goods to the camp, John Kermode's company must have been kept very busy.

KNOCKALOE INTERNMENT CAMP

Three very well-dressed internees posing for the camera.
Despite having nowhere to go, appearances were maintained.

100 YEARS OF HISTORY

Two smart detainees with their camp dog. Many stray cats and dogs were adopted by the camp inhabitants.

Picture postcards showing detainees putting on a gymnastics display during a German Gymnastics Festival day. The well known exercise Pilates was created by Joseph Pilates during his internment in Knockaloe.

Above: Wardens, seated, watching the sporting events unfold at the Gymnastics Festival.

Left: Another form of exercise was formal marching as seen in this display.

KNOCKALOE INTERNMENT CAMP

Right: Close shot of detainees showing their gymnastic skills on the parallel bars.

Below: Some of the internees who formed this 'Turn Verein' or gymnastics club posing with several guards who are standing at ease for the photograph.

100 YEARS OF HISTORY

Detail of rare Jewish picture postcard sent from Jos Sibor P.O.W. 15809, camp III hut 6 b. Inset shows full card.

22   KNOCKALOE INTERNMENT CAMP

Above: A watercolour painting on a postcard by O. Jasob, dated 1915. The dark colours and brooding atmosphere really give a sense of what the camp was like in the evenings.

Right: Reverse of card with a Christmas greeting for 1915.

100 YEARS OF HISTORY 23

One of the cards that began Stephen's collection. Colour hand-tinted art card by G. Stol showing an aerial view of the camp with Peel Castle in the distance. Celebrating Christmas 1915, the text reads:

The war drags on and yet the sprig of Love
Stays green throughout the Winter
A star winks announcing peace
Throughout the Night
True Greetings from Knockaloe camp

Snowy landscape art card by A. Gerssel from Christmas 1915 sent by P.O.W. 15918 headed 'Glory to God in the highest and peace on earth' and offering warm Christmas wishes from the camp community and Pastor R. Hartmann. Perhaps the landscape glimpsed in the distance could be seen from the camp? Note the beautiful art nouveau floral border which would have been very current at the time.

100 YEARS OF HISTORY

Another beautifully rendered decorative line drawing by G.C. Stoltz, this Christmas card with camp Pastor Hartmann's name at the bottom features a poem:

I dared boldly to lift my head
despite the winters threat
Is there no end to
the winter – no renewal
of the earth?
I shyly rubbed my eyes – there shines a light!
Be courageous and
look! Do I recognize this fir tree?
It warms me and makes me merry
and says "The native sun soon wins!
Be my messenger, don't lose time!
That's why I start to bloom, full of delight!"
Hear the message of the "Christ-Rose"
For my friends at Knockaloe for the 3rd Christmas.
R. Hartmann - Pastor

C.

GOVERNMENT OFFICE,
ISLE OF MAN.

19th March 1915.

Any further communication on the subject of this letter should be addressed to—
The Government Secretary,
   Government Office,
      Isle of Man,
and the following number quoted:—

This is to certify that Pastor Hartmann is employed on the Staff of Knockaloe Detention Camp, Isle of Man. He is travelling to Birmingham to his congregation after which he will return to the Isle of Man.

Government Secretary.

Opposite: A chalk drawing depicting Pastor Hartmann, mentioned on both previous cards. He was pastor in the camp until October 1917 when, after several requests, he was repatriated due to the death of his brother and the ill health of his mother. Unusually Pastor Hartmann was allowed to leave the camp, and indeed the Island, on occasions to attend to his congregation in England (see below).

Left: Interesting letter allowing Pastor Hartmann to travel outside the camp, to his congregation at a Lutheran church in Birmingham.

KNOCKALOE INTERNMENT CAMP

The first page of a sermon for lost comrades, one of the collection of letters Stephen has, many of which still need to be translated. See opposite page for translation of this letter. The detainees that died in Knockaloe were buried in Patrick church.

Heroes' Blood

Do you hear the stream trickling at night?
It is the blood that's flowing home,
Of enemies beige after a violent fight,
Where national heroes were slain*.

It runs off helmets, trickles down steel
Until one brook feeds into another
From princes to farmers, cadet, general
Their lifeblood mingles and seeps into the ground.

Soon all this land's roots will be red
And the foot touch holy ground.
No mourning dresses do widows wear
And stranger greet one another.

They gave their husbands, gave their kids
Their blood is flowing through people and country
It seeps through the empire's dykes and sinks,
Pulses house to house, wall to wall.

Dear friends. We are gathered here together to observe Totensonntag† in a way we have never done before. May we never see another day like this, when we have to hold a ceremony under the same circumstances, for we cannot and must not express our emotions but in the depths of our hearts. Except for the quiet funeral we held last week, when we lowered one of our comrades into the ground out in the peaceful churchyard, which now holds so many of ours. At this hour we wistfully and sorrowfully remember our dead, especially the flocks from our midst, the young and old, who will never again see home because they have been lead to the greater home. Today we should focus on the challenging task to prepare a worthy burial ground for our dead. But our dead here in Knockaloe, those are just the few thousand who will return home, who will once again be allowed to live. Our dead are the others over there, who will not be granted a return, whom we will never see and never be able to embrace again; our friends, our brothers, our sons, our fathers, and we; we're helpless, far away, cut off, lonesome, imprisoned. But today is Sunday of the Dead, and we are allowed to commemorate them, and in our thoughts we want to see them again before us, in all their youthfulness, all their seriousness, all their love. We want to pledge allegiance to them with the best we have and that bound us to them: You friends, you brothers, you sons, you fathers, you are lost to us, but in the depths of our hearts you live on (…)

(Translation by Laura M. Wenzlaw)

* lit.: fell
† German-Lutheran holiday on which congregations commemorate fallen soldiers and the dead in general.

Christmas 1915.
A commemorative poem, with direct feeling about the war and its effects. By the end of 1915 the war was fully underway and the enormity of the conflict was beginning to be felt by both sides. The panel at the bottom illustrates a German war grave at the front. The border of thorns may symbolise the plight of the prisoners at Knockaloe. Translation opposite.

Christmas joy — Christmas cheer?

Joy, withdraw yourself, cheer, hide yourself!

Christmas is shrouded in grief today
The world is in pain
Who could possibly feel joy on this day,
Who dares to spread cheer?
All hearts unite to proclaim
A lamentation, sad and low
Up to the Heavens, down to earth
Songs of sorrow, not of joy are sung
Heaven's gates are locked
Blood is shed in torrents
It screams to heaven, loudly screaming
It screams into the Christmas night
Mingled with (the whole world's?) tears
It rises up to the Heavens,
Seeps deep into the earth
Lamenting and wailing, moaning and keening

Mothers', brides' and orphans' tears,
Fathers', sons' and old men's blood
Ascend—the world's cry for help—
To heaven, declaring their pain.

But I hear the heaven's choir
From up above a roaring cheer
The angel armies loudly proclaiming:
"We bring you peace, we bring you the Bride,
We lead to you the KING OF CREATION*,
'Peace on earth', peace and quiet."
He is preparing himself, he's ready
He enters the furious fray.
He approaches in Heavenly majesty,
Behold he stand on glowing clouds.
He is coming to rightfully judge the peoples
And the earth will bow before him.
At his mouth's powerful wrath
The world's fiery fount will dry out
And hell and its power will flee
And all dark creatures will run and hide

Death is swallowed up, HIS IS THE VICTORY,
Away with the tears, with blood and war;
He has taken over command,
CHRIST IS KING, HIS KINGDOM'S COME.

Christmas joy — Christmas cheer? —
Joy, emerge, cheer, break forth!
Sing with the heavenly choir:
"Glory to God in the highest, and on earth";—
Sorrow changes into joy, into cheer.—
Heavenly peace, heavenly quiet
Approaches on angels' wings.

Dedicated to his dear compatriots and fellow prisoners of war.

(Translation by Laura M. Wenzlaw)

* lit.: King of Honor

Above: This photograph showing some of the detainees' graves at Patrick church. In 1962 most of the detainees were re-buried at Cannock Chase in England. Two Jewish and several Turkish graves still remain at Patrick church.

Opposite: A prayer in the style of a poem, on a postcard, by Ebenezer Elliott. This was most likely used for a sermon.

4. GOD SAVE THE PEOPLE.

When wilt Thou save the people?
  O God of Mercy, when?
The people, Lord, the people,
  Not thrones and crowns, but men!
Flowers of Thy heart, O God, are they;
Let them not pass, like weeds, away—
Their heritage a sunless day,
            God save the people!

Shall crime bring crime for ever—
  Strength aiding still the strong?
Is it Thy Will, O Father,
  That man shall toil for wrong?
"No," say Thy mountains, "No," Thy skies;
Man's clouded sun shall brightly rise,
And songs ascend instead of sighs,
            God save the people!

When wilt Thou save the people?
  O God of Mercy, when?
The people, Lord, the people,
  Not thrones and crowns, but men!
God save the people; Thine they are,
Thy children, as Thine angels fair;
From vice, oppression, and despair,
            God save the people!

                    EBENEZER ELLIOTT.

This page and opposite: These picture postcards show some of the many items being produced in the camp. These items were for sale and were available for public perusal at camp open days. Notably, many picture frames were carved in the camp. The variety of items and ingenuity of the inmates can be appreciated when looking at the goods offered for sale at these camp craft fairs.

100 YEARS OF HISTORY   35

The photographs above and left show models of gun carriages, model ships, carved boxes, picture frames, hand mirrors, ships in bottles and fabrics for sale. More interesting perhaps is the effort put into dressing up for these occasions – everyone is turned out immaculately.

More items for sale.

Below: Two picture frames from Stephen's collection made by the inmates of Knockaloe. The photographs are most likely the maker's children.

100 YEARS OF HISTORY 37

Further items for sale, including model locomotives, ships and pieces of art.

KNOCKALOE INTERNMENT CAMP

Above: An advert for the selling of items made in the camp which would have included items on the previous pages, as well as what is pictured above right.

Right: A box which was made in the camp, six dice which are made out of animal bone and two attendance medals which were made out of the metal liners of tea chests.

100 YEARS OF HISTORY 39

Inset picture postcard of the many bone items that were produced. Stephen owns four of these items, three vases, two of which are a matching set, and a pin cushion. The bones were collected after meals, boiled down so that marrow could be removed and then carved.

KNOCKALOE INTERNMENT CAMP

Art pieces were also for sale. This softly shaded pencil drawing is by P.O.W. 1813, camp I and sold for 5/- a dozen.

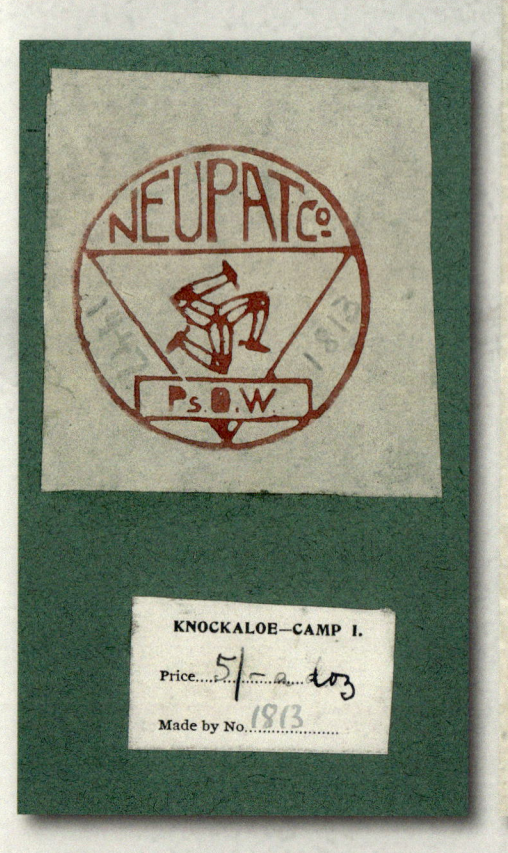

100 YEARS OF HISTORY   41

A larger example of P.O.W. 1813's artwork.

A silver brooch made from silver coins, depicting scenes from both Douglas and Knockaloe camps, the maker's initials in the middle: possibly made by or for somebody who may have lived in both camps during WW1.

100 YEARS OF HISTORY

A postcard sent into the camp to a Mr Bauer P.O.W. 5418 compound I camp I, from his daughter Minnie. In the text she talks about Laurence expecting to be called up any day, ironically, to fight the Germans.

KNOCKALOE INTERNMENT CAMP

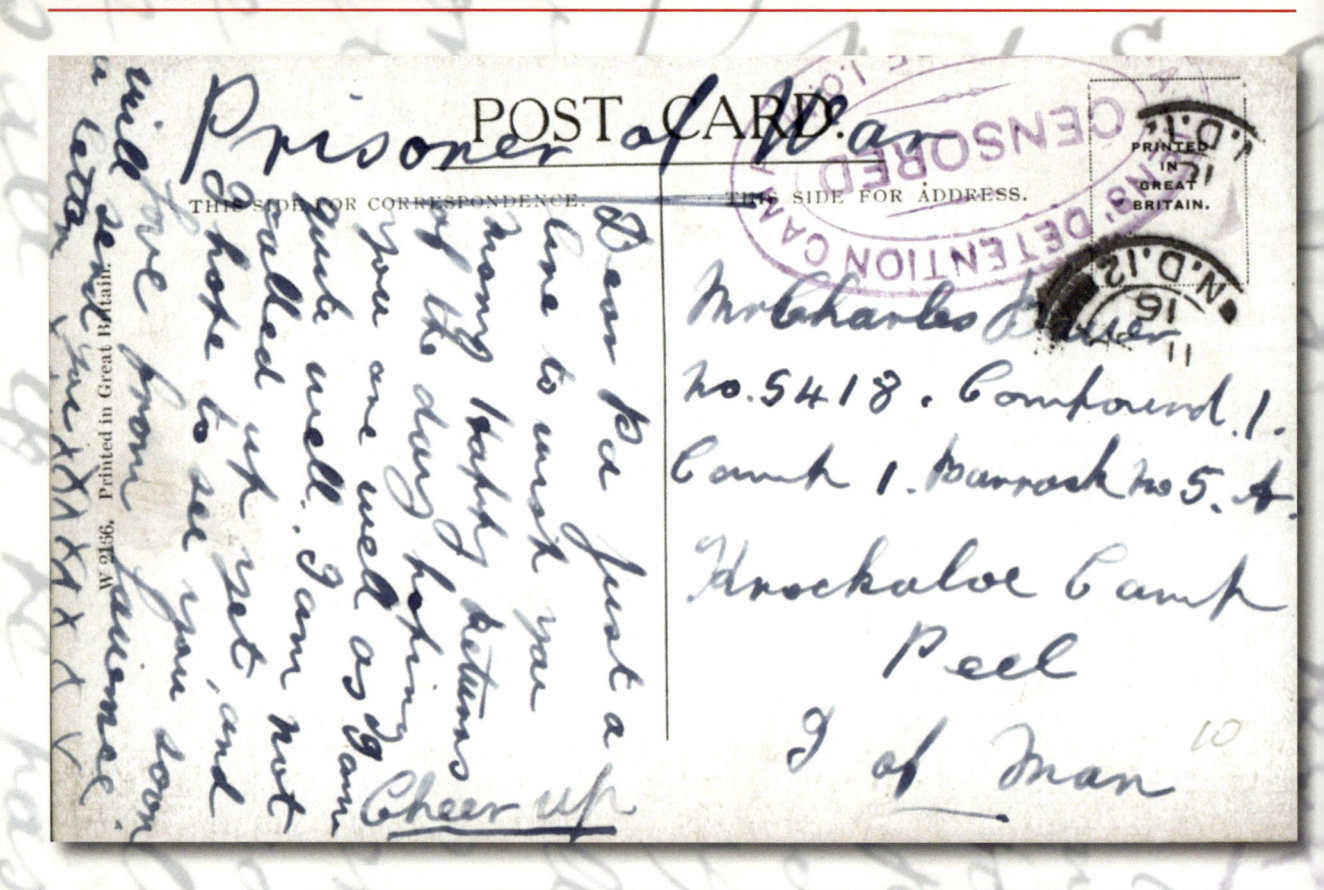

Above: postcard birthday wishes from Laurence.

Right: card birthday wishes from Ma and Sophie.

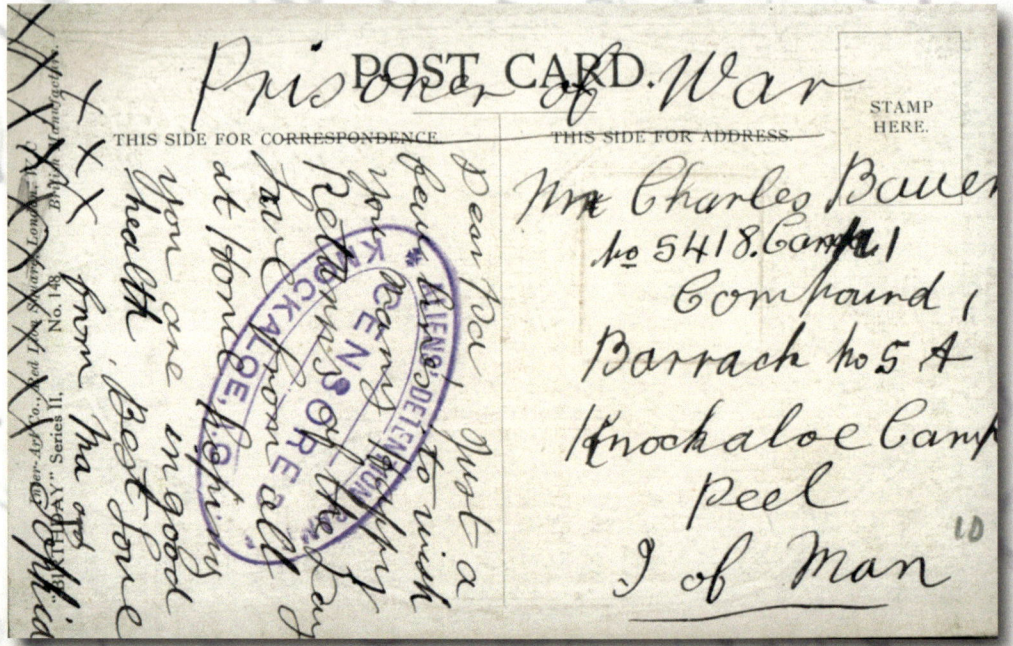

100 YEARS OF HISTORY   45

Minnie writes once again to her father, explaining none of the boys have been called up yet but Laurence has joined up as he was compelled to. These postcards tell a story yet to be discovered. Whether he returned is unknown.

All correspondence entering or leaving the camp was examined and stamped by the official censor.

Camp theatre sheet from 1914-1915 for a production of 'Old Heidelberg' featuring lovely artwork and evocative images of home but also weaving in various Manx iconography. Note the cherubim on the right riding a chariot which is apparently being pulled by a Manx cat.

100 YEARS OF HISTORY   47

OKTOBER-FEST 1916
KRIEGSGEFANGENEN-LAGER KNOCKALOE, CAMP I

INSELMAN

ARRANGIERT
VOM
FUSSBALL - VERBAND
CAMP I.

Reservierter Stuhl. st. I.

Football programme cover designed by A Gensel for the camp's Oktober Fest for 1916. Sporting events were regularly staged at Knockaloe.

16. HINDERNISLAUFEN ueber 800 Meter. offen fuer jedermann.

13 Oezwirk	55 Maeder	102 Galwos
15 Wellinger	63 Kunz	108 Henk
39 Crauss	66 Steiniger	128 Reith
70 Jungnickel	64 Vogl	127 Froeck
57 Dreyer, Josef	74 Friedel	138 Wolf
56 Dreyer, Anton	75 Schneider, Georg	82 Korn

Sieges aus den Vorlaeufen..

Sieger aus dem Endlauf 1. *74*   2. *13*   3. *15*

17. LAUFEN FUER DIE MUSICKAPELLE ueber 200 Meter.

Floete	Cornett I	Cornett IV	Tenor	Grosse Trommel
Clarinette I	„ II	Horn I	Posune	Kleine Trommel
„ II	„ III	„ II	Bass	

Sieger.................................

18. TROSTRENNEN fuer diejenigen, welche in keinem der vorhergehenden Rennen gesiegt haben (1500 Meter).

Sieger...... *138* ....

III. Fussball um die Meisterschaft des Lagers Knockaloe

(nur Endspiel, am gweiten Tage).

Compound I.	Compound II.	Compound III	Compound V	Compound VI
Frohnhoefer (Kapt)	Kleinagel (Kapt)	Karstaedt (Kapt)	Galwos (Kapt)	Wagner (Kapt)
Schwartz	Mueller	Boeckenhauer	Kuhr	Schulze
Obermayer	Arens	Bachus	Heinemann	Golzer
Stang	Dehn	Paerschke	Parth	Gensel
Leineweber	Wilcke	Bischoff	Berschke	Meinecke
Jagusch	Stowasser	Wetzel	Henk	Niersch
Tschuertz	Mallinckrodt	Rivers	Tunge	Stein
Bauer	Henry	Baasch	Schneider, Max	Spahr
Zelle	Wackermann	Phendt	Lorenz	Thies
Berner	Sejbold	Schiller	Warnecke	Wieske
Ziegler	Ernst	Blumenthal	Maier	Suess

Sieger..................................

IV. Preisverteilung

100 YEARS OF HISTORY   49

Above: Picture postcard of the Compound 5 football team 1916.

Left: Picture of football team from compound 5 with names included. When Stephen and Rosalind were searching through material to include in this book, it was only then they discovered that some names on the card matched those in the programme. Both items were purchased from different sources so it was a nice surprise that they matched up.

KNOCKALOE INTERNMENT CAMP

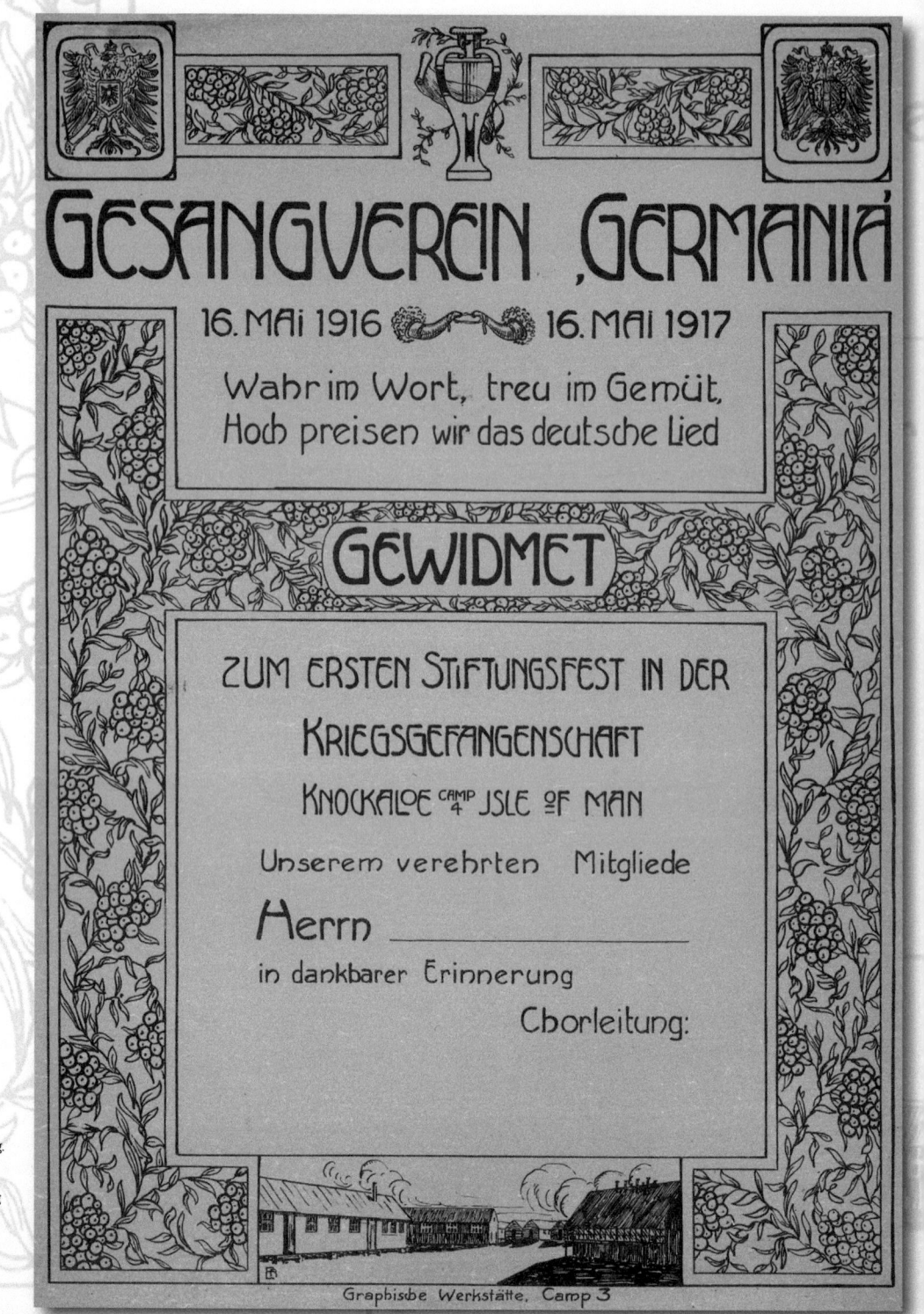

A singing club certificate for the German Choral Society event in which nationalist songs were sung. Featuring some elegant floral work and German symbolism, it was printed in the graphic workshop of Camp 3. It reads under the date:

Truth to the word and faithful to the mind we highly praise the German song. Dedicated

The first celebration of the trust during imprisonment in Knockaloe Camp IV Isle of Man. Our honoured member Mr_____

In grateful remembrance.

GESANGVEREIN „GERMANIA"

16. MAI 1916 — 16. MAI 1917

Wahr im Wort, treu im Gemüt,
Hoch preisen wir das deutsche Lied

GEWIDMET

ZUM ERSTEN STIFTUNGSFEST IN DER
KRIEGSGEFANGENSCHAFT
KNOCKALOE CAMP 4 ISLE OF MAN

Unserem verehrten Mitgliede

Herrn _____

in dankbarer Erinnerung

Chorleitung:

Graphische Werkstätte, Camp 3

Charity Concert for the improvement and maintenance of the graves of prisoners who died while in British internment camps, held by the choir "Harmonie" in 1916. Drawn by A. Steinkamp.

Prog

I. Teil.

1. **Chor:** Wie sie so sanft ruhn. — F. W. Beneken.

2. Ansprache. Herr. H. Weber.

3. **Chor:**
   (a) „Sie sollen ihn nicht haben" — Schumann.
   (b) „Du Schwert an meiner Linken" — M. v. Weber.

4. **Gedicht Vortr.** Marinebilder. Herr E. Kauslund. — Meves.
   (a) „Auf nach China" — Matrosenl. V.1.
   (b) „Jm Taifun" (Jltisuntergang) — Chor: „ V.2.
   (c) „Hoch" — Stolz weht.

5. Keulenschwingen vom Turnverein.

6. **Gedicht Vortr.** „Ein Heldentod." Herr E. Wezel. — Julie Ludwig.
   Chor: „Morgenrot." — G. Wohlgemuth.

7. „ „ „Mutterliebe." Herr E. Probst. — Franz Meyer.

---

10 Minuten Pause.

Es wird dringend gebeten, das Rauchen zu unterlassen!

The inside programme for the May Concert, listing the players and the pieces they performed. Patrons are requested to refrain from smoking.

II. Teil.

8. Gedicht Vort.   „Pardonniert."   Herr H. Weber.   Graf Wickenburg.
   Chor: „Es geht bei gedaempft.   F. Silcher.

9.   Pyramiden vom Turnverein.

10. Chor: (a) „Jch hatt' einen Kameraden."   F. Silcher.
   (b) „Stumm schlaeft der Saenger."   F. Silcher.

11. Gedicht Votr.   „Ob Freund, ob Freund." Herr H. Volk.   Gust. Bode.
   Chor: Wielange soll ich noch fern dir sein.
   F. Moehring.

12. Leb. Bild.   „Kriegers Sterben."   Hen. Meineweh.
   Ein Verwundeter,   Herr Burczack.
   Ein Unteroffizier,   Herr Schilling.
   Zwei Soldaten,   Probst u. Wiebach.

13. Chor: „Fuer Uns."   G. Schreck.

Die Gesammteinnahme wird dem Friedhof Fond überwiesen.

Maenner Chor „Harmonie" Comp v. Camp 1.

Dirigent Herr Carl Mehnert.

Ackermann.	Hempel.	Schilling.
Ballhorn.	Herzog.	Schmidt.
Bartl.	Holder.	Schreiber.
Bauerfeind.	Huber.	Schulz.
Bernhard.	Kauslund.	Senk.
Bluemer.	Kuhr.	Steffens.
Brunner.	Kurz.	Teubner.
Burczack.	Lange.	Thiem.
Fromme.	Middel.	Volk.
Grosse.	Probst.	Weber.
Griehshammer.	Rumbold.	Wezel.
Heinemann.	Rübelmann.	Wiebach.
Zier.	Zimmermann.	

Pyramiden.

Leiter Herr M. Schroeder.

1. E. de Buhr.
2. C. Stachelhaus.
3. E. Probst.
4. L. Fischer.
5. R. Petzold.
6. S. Biedinger.
7. M. Genolles.
8. H. Aumann.
9. H. Pfeil.
10. A. Hattendorf.
11. O. Schoepf.
12. F. Tunger.
13. H. Hayen.
14. M. Donaykowski.
15. P. Arnold.
16. F. Kampmüller.
17. M. Kaden.
18. S. Vesler.
19. K. Scholle.
20. W. Mensing.

Keulenschwingen.

1. S. Uesler.
2. H. Schwetje.
3. S. Biedinger.
4. H. Sellmann.
5. R. Petzold.

Vorstand.

Carl Mehnert.
Musikal Leiter.

Heinrich Weber.
I. Vors.

M. Schroeder.
II. Vors.

Alois Middel.
Kass.

Eduard Kauslund.
I. Vors. d. M.C. „H."

Heinrich Volk.
II. Vors. d.M.C. „H."

W. J. Clarke, Printer, Peel.

100 YEARS OF HISTORY

KNOCKALOE CAMP - THEATER.

Camp 1.   Compound 2.

Donnerstag, den 1. Juni, 1916.

GROSSES ---
Wohlthaetigkeits-Konzert

des

THEATER ORCHESTERS

zu Gunsten

der Kranken und zur Erhaltung der Graeber

Dirigent: R. STERBAL.

Geschaeftsleitung: Der Kranken und Begraebniss Ausschuss.

Anfang 7-30.

Programm.

1. FACKELTANZ ... ... Meyerbeer
2. OUVERTURE "FREISCHUETZ" ... ... Weber
3. PEER GYNT SUITE 2 ... ... Grieg
   (a) BRAUTRAUB—INGRIDS KLAGE
   (b) PEER GYNTS HEIMKEHR
   (c) SOLVEJGS LIED
4. TRIO:
   (a) LARGHETTO ... ... Dyff
   (b) AVE MARIA ... ... Bach-Gounod

(Violine: R. Sterbal; Cello: W. Langenstrass; Pianoforte: W. Baumfelder)

— PAUSE —

5. REMINISCENZEN AN SCHUBERT ... ... Berger
6. NOCTURNE ... ... Mendelssohn
7. BLUMENGEFLUESTER ... ... Blon
8. UNGARISCHE RHAPSODIE 2 ... ... Liszt

W. J. CLARKE, Printer 35, Michael Street, Peel.

Another benefit concert, this time for the benefit of the sick and the preservation of graves. This programme sheet from camp I theatre, compound 2 promotes the concert of classical pieces on Thursday 1 June 1916. Printed by W.J. Clarke, Printer, 35 Michael Street, Peel rather than inside the camp printing workshops.

KNOCKALOE INTERNMENT CAMP

Beautiful card written in gold leaf dated 1916. It quotes John 6:68: 'Lord, to whom shall we go? You have the words of eternal life.' And reads: With best wishes, S. C. Gauntlett.

100 YEARS OF HISTORY

4/8/16.

Lieber Herr Pastor!

Habe ich Ihnen eigentlich schon geschrieben, dass ich vor 3 Wochen Ihren Freund Korth begrüsste? Es geht ihm ganz gut und er hofft dasselbe von Ihnen. Ich soll Ihnen herzliche Grüsse bestellen. Diesen füge ich mich an. Sie werden wohl jetzt gerade etwas besseres Wetter haben. Soll regne hie reichlich. Ich hoffe Mitte September im Lager zu sein. Auf Wiedersehn!

Ihr […]

Reverse of card with camp stamp and dated 4/8/16.

Theater-Halle – Compound 1. (Camp I).

Großer Bazaar.   Sonntag, den 23. Juli 1916

PROGRAMM.

1. "Kriegs-Marsch" .... M. Lutschow
2. "Siebenboten-Walzer" .... Blankenburg
3. "Krausköpfchen", Salonstück .... Silvestel
4. "Alplers Frühlingsjubel" Ländler ... Kusse
5. Humoristische Vorträge .... Leman
6. "Kriegsmarsch in Triester" .... Mendelssohn
7. "Knallbonbons", Potpourri .... Morena
8. "Esmeralda" Spanisches Intermezzo .. Krüger
9. "Deutschlands Zukunft" Marsch ...... Kruse

Buffet:

Kaffee .... 1 d
Streuselkuchen .... 1 d
Gefüllter Kuchen .... 1½ d
~~Schokoladen Torte~~ .... ~~1½ d~~
Pudding .... 2 d
~~Apfelwein pro Glas~~ .... ~~1½ d~~
     dto. Flasche .... 9 d
Aprikosen-Limonade p. Glas .... 1½ d
     dto. dto. p. Flasche .... 9 d
Obst, Zigarren, Zigaretten

Andenken für Sammler

Theatre program compound I camp I for Sunday 23 July 1916. As well as offering a buffet, it features an unusual Manx cat stamp on the programme with 'Souvenirs for collectors' stamped on it. The stamp itself is a very detailed woodcut print produced in 1915 in one of the camp workshops. It shows a set of woodcarving tools and a shield with Manx triskellion.

Weihnachts-Winterfest des Turnverein „Jahn"

Knockaloe, Camp 1, Compound 1, d. 16 und 17 Dezember, 1916,
6-45 Abends.

unter guetiger Mitwirkung des BUEHNENVEREINS Compound I.

Musik: THEATERORCHESTER Compound I.

Dirigent: Max Niemeyer.

VORSTAND DES TURNVEREIN "JAHN."

Vorsitzender: C. Richard-Mylius.   Turnwarte: W. Scherer, W. Bajohr, A. Gerisch.
Vorturner: R. Schmidt, O. Kunzendorf, K. Schneider, F. Ziegler, E. Jagsch.
Geraetewart: Th. Arntz.   Kassierer: R. Schumacher.   Schriftfuehrer: C. Noggler.

Programm

1. Eroeffnungsmarsch.
2. Begruessung der Gaeste.
3. Spezial-Freiuebungen.
4. Die beiden Meteore Fred und Fritz.
5. Kuerturnen am Barren.
6. Keulenschwingen.
7. Fahnenreigen mit Blitzstabuebungen.

"PAUSE."

8. **Lottchens Geburtstag**
   Lustspiel in einem Aufzug von L. Thoma.

   PERSONEN.
   Geh. Rat Dr. Otto Giselius,
       Uuiversitaetsprofessor ... Herr Bossert
   Mathilde, seine Frau ... ... „ Schuetzke
   Lottchen, beider Tochter ... ... „ Bischof
   Coolestine Giselius, Schwester des
       Geheimrats ... ... „ A. Jaeger
   Dr. Traugott Appel, Privatdozent ... „ Thieme
   Babette, Koechin bei Giselius ... „ Reininger

   Ort d. Handlung: Kl. Universitaetsstadt.
   Zeit: Gegenwart.

9. Kuerturnen am Reck.
10. Parterreturnen (8 Clown).
11. Pferd-Pyramiden.
12. Schlussmarsch.

GUT HEIL.

W. J. CLARKE, Printer, 55, Michael Street, Peel.

A Christmas winter festival programme. A celebration of sports club "Jahn". Music, theatre and orchestra events programmed and the heads of the club are mentioned. "Tunverein" was a nationalist group. The progamme also includes acrobatics, gymnastics with clowns, vaulting horse work and ends with a display of marching.

KNOCKALOE INTERNMENT CAMP

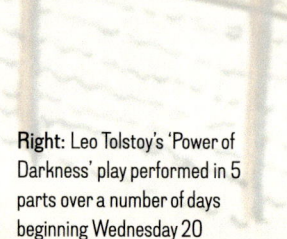

KLEINES THEATER
COMP. 6.

Mittwoch den 20. Dezember, 1916
und folgende Tage.

Die Macht der Finsternis

Drama in 5 Aufzuegen
von
Lew Nikolaiewicz Tolstoy.

Beginn 6-15 Abends.

TOLSTOY WOCHE.

Right: Leo Tolstoy's 'Power of Darkness' play performed in 5 parts over a number of days beginning Wednesday 20 December 1916 in a programme of events labelled as Tolstoy Week..

Opposite: Christmas Festival programme, camp III compound 5. Some of the internees were obviously well-versed in the art of calligraphy as this elegant programme cover demonstrates.

Knockaloe-Lager
Camp 3, Comp. 5.

Fest-Programm

Weihnachten
1916.

Weihnachtsfeier

Sonntag, d. 24. Dezember 1916. abends 5½ Uhr.

1. Largo ...... (von F. Händel) .... Salon-Orchester
2. Gemeinsamer Gesang .... Stille Nacht!
3. Ansprache .... Herr M. Horner
4. a) O du fröhliche . Männer-Chor
   b) Tochter Zion .... F. Händel
   (Männer-Chor u. Orchester)
5. Gemeinsamer Gesang:
   Gedenkt der Brüder im Felde.

This page and opposite: The inside of this Christmas Eve programme for 1916 features a lovely drawing of Saint Nikolas and more oustanding examples of penmanship in the lettering. During Monday 25th and Tuesday 26th of December, the ambitious programme over four acts takes place initially in a city followed by the second, third and fourth acts which take place in a lonely castle in a mountainous region. Produced in the camp's graphic workshop.

Fest-Aufführung

Montag, d. 25. u. Dienstag, d. 26. Dezembr. 1916.
abends 6½ Uhr.

Alexandra

Drama in vier Aufzügen. v. Rich. Voss

Personen:

Frau Präsidentin v. Eberti	Herr Stermann
Erwin, ihr Sohn	" Hagedorn
Alexandra	" Koch
Dr. Andrea, Rechtsanwalt	" Kuntze
Ant. Möll, Förster a. d. Gute d. Präsidentin	" Bungs
Bauer Gerland	" Überschaar
Frau Lemm, Besitzerin eines eleg. Hotel garni.	" Reiche
Ein Arzt	" Rössler
Portier	" Heinemann
Christoph, im Dienste d. Präsidentin	" Theodor

Der erste Aufzug spielt in einer grossen Stadt,
der zweite, dritte u. vierte auf einem einsamen
Schlosse in einer Gebirgsgegend.

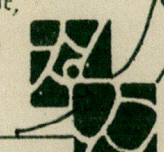

Graphische Werkstätte.

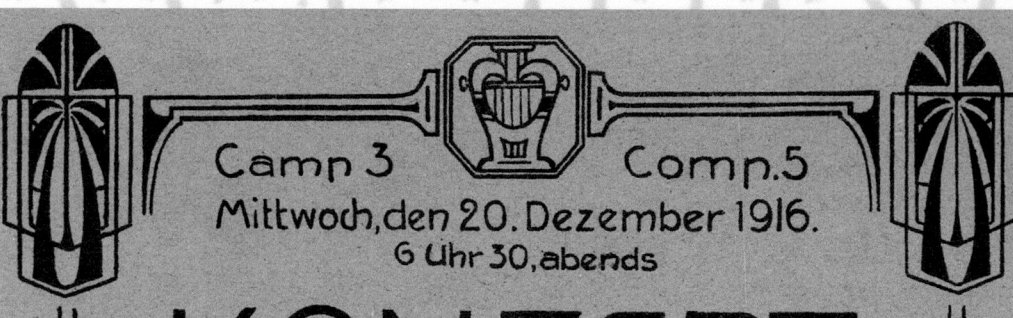

Camp 3   Comp. 5
Mittwoch, den 20. Dezember 1916.
6 Uhr 30, abends

KONZERT

des

Salon-Orchesters

Hans Scheuffler.

MUSIK – FOLGE

1. Teil.

1. Marsch a.d. Oper „Tannhäuser" Einzug d. Gäste   R. Wagner
2. Ouverture z. Oper „Titus"   W.A. Mozart
3. Andante a.d. „Unvollendeten Sinfonie in H moll"   Fr. Schubert
4. Sinfonie № 12 in B dur   a) Lento b) Allegro vivace
   c) Adagio d) Menuett e) Presto   Jos. Haydn

2. Teil.

5. Ouverture z. Op. „Die Jtalienerin in Algier"   G. Rossini
6. Männer-Chor Comp. 5 (Dirigent H. Scheuffler)
   a) Weihe d. Gesanges (Priesterchor a. „Die Zauberflöte"   W.A. Mozart
   b) Heimkehr (E. Schimpke)   J. Gelbke
   c) Heimatland (L. Heller) für 8 stimm. Männer-Chor   Ant. Dressler
7. Walzer „An der schönen blauen Donau"   Joh. Strauss
8. Fantasie a.d. Oper „Preciosa"   C.M. v. Weber
9. Soldaten-Chor a.d. Oper „Faust"
   (für Männer-Chor und Orchester)   Ch. Gounod

Graphische-Werkstätte Camp. 3.

This flyer advertises a concert of Musical Episodes to be held on 20th December 1916 at 6.30 in camp III compound 5. Produced in the graphic workshop of camp 3.

100 YEARS OF HISTORY 65

Art card drawn by F.W. Kehrhahn. The scene depicts a vision of Christmas at home set against the reality of the camp interior after four years of internment. The barbed wire border evocatively symbolises the loss of freedom of the internees. The card was sent by Joseph Huber, P.O.W. 2527, camp I compound 3.

KNOCKALOE INTERNMENT CAMP

Herzliche Weihnachts- und Neujahrswünsche

Weihnachten
von O.Mi

Glocken schwingen im Raum. Vieles hat uns getrennt.
Singen zur Ruhe die Schmerzen. Vieles uns innig verbunden.
Liebste, entzünde die Kerzen Trübe und selige Stunden,
Nun am festlichen Baum! Stunden, die keiner sonst kennt.

Still wird heute der Schmerz,
Und in den heiligen Frieden,
Den ans die Liebe beschieden,
Sinkst du mir schweigend ans Herz.

Aus der KRIEGSGEFANGENSCHAFT
KNOCKALOE, INSEL MAN
DEZEMBER 1916

Christmas postcard 1916 the man deep in thought about his family at home during the Christmas period. The poem tells of the pain of being away from home but asks those back home to light the candles on the Christmas tree.

100 YEARS OF HISTORY   67

Weihnachten 1916.

Oh gold'ne Weihnachtszeit!
Mich zieht mein Sinn
Mit tausend Banden heut
Zur Heimat hin.

Mir strahlt im Lichterglanz
Ein Tannenbaum,
Der Mutter Weihnachtslied
Klingt mir im Traum.

Ich sinne träumend hin
In Sehnsuchtsqual --
Von fern tönt Glockenklang
Es war einmal.

Max Horner.

Left: Christmas 1916 poem speaks of a golden Christmas time and how strongly the author's senses and thoughts are drawn towards his homeland. In his mind's eye he sees a Christmas tree and many lights, in his dreams he hears his mother singing Christmas carols. He dreamingly thinks about it in agony and hears bells ringing from far away.

Below: Another excellent 3 colour printed card by Behrens. The dates on Santa's sack run from 1914 to 1917 with a question mark indicating that another year may await internees in the future.

Weihnachtsgrüsse a.d. Zivilgefangenenlager Knockaloe, I.o.M.

Calendar printed in the camp, dated 1917. Notice Corrins Tower in the background of the scene. The German Imperial Eagle watches over the year and the fanastic stylised cloud formations have been rendered in a woodcut style in pen and ink.

100 YEARS OF HISTORY   69

Another fine New Year celebration illustration by G. Stoltz. The card calls for Peace in 1917 and offers warmest wishes for the New Year from Knockaloe.

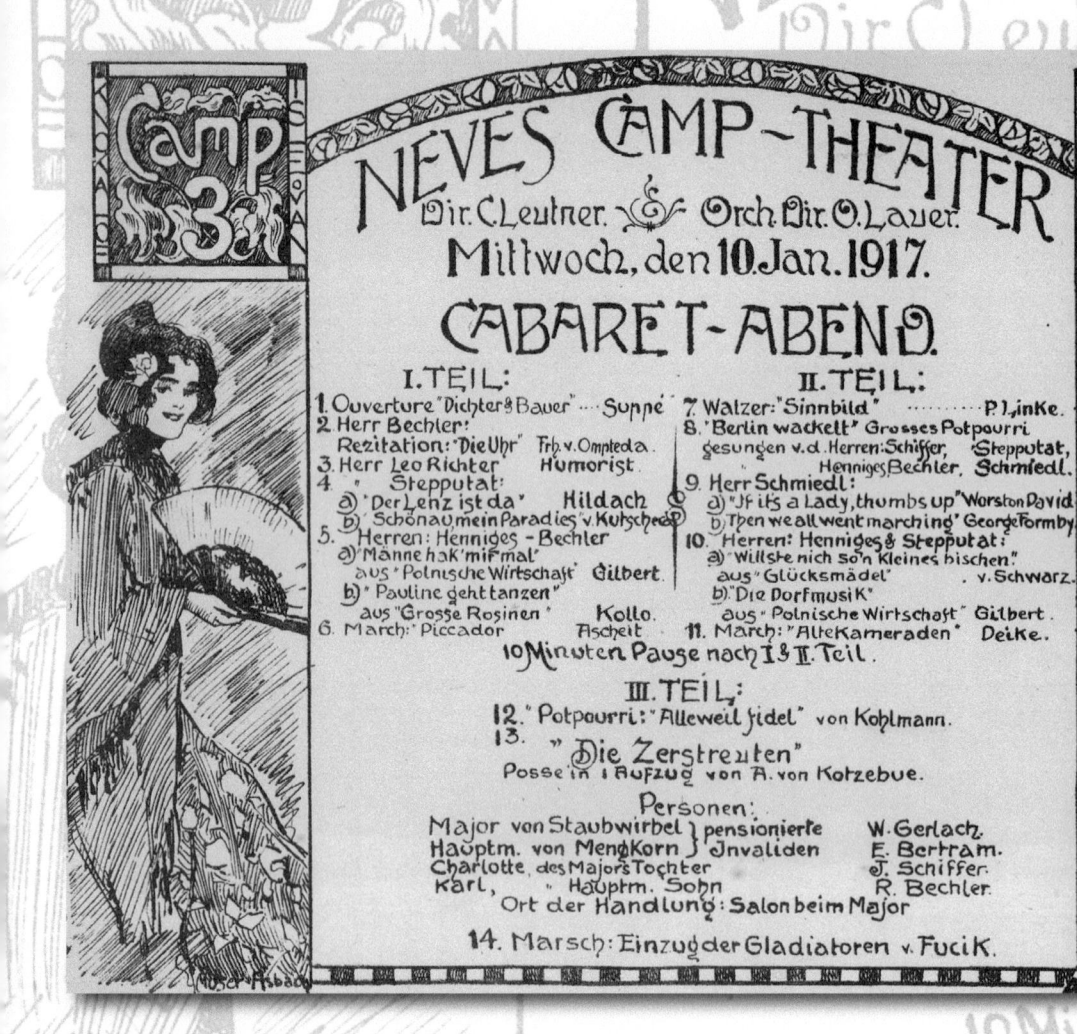

Advertising flyer from the Camp Theatre promoting a cabaret evening on Wednesday 10 January 1917. Despite being interned for so many years, the inmates were still putting on entertainment for the other residents. The evening promised singing, dancing, music and comedy.

100 YEARS OF HISTORY 71

·FRÖHLICHE·

·OSTERN·

KNOCKALOE-CAMP ISLE OF MAN·

Happy Easter from Knockaloe Camp with this delightfully drawn and colourfully printed card. The dove of peace leaves the top of the egg while lower down the pussy willows signal the beginning of spring, all set against the huts of the camp lower down.

KNOCKALOE INTERNMENT CAMP

An Easter card which talks of how far the sound of the homeland's bells travel today, how strong their sound, fanfares sing joyfully, like always the passages of arms are found. It goes on to say that the truth of the Easter saga tells them that even in hurt they should join the strength of Wotan's (another name for Norse-god Odin) beautiful spring days back home.

100 YEARS OF HISTORY

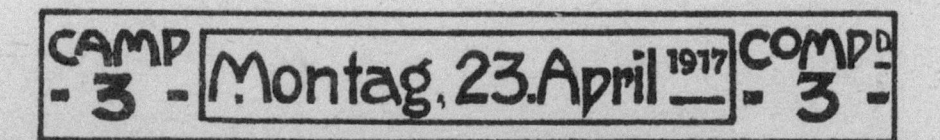

CAMP 3 — Montag, 23. April 1917 — COMPD 3

GROSSES KONZERT
DIREKTION: OTTO LAUER

MUSIK-FOLGE

1. Marsch "Abschied der Gladiatoren" — Blankenburg
2. Ouverture "Maurer und Schlosser" — Auber
3. Walzer "Wiener Blut" — Joh. Strauss
4. Violin-Solo "Romanze" (Herr Schmidt) — Wilhelmy
5. Militär-Symphonie — Haydn
   a. Adagio — b. Allegro — c. Allegretto — d. Menuett — e. Finale Presto
6. 2 Ungarische Tänze No 5 u. 6 — Brahms

PAUSE

7. Ouverture "Prinz von Oranien" — C. Latann
8. Walzer "Die Schlittschuhläufer" — Waldteufel
9. Fantasie "Romaneska" — Zikoff
10. "Tannhäusers Erzählung" / "Sigmunds Liebeslied" aus "Walküre" — R. Wagner
    Tenor-Solo: Herr Wagschal
11. Grosses Potpourri aus "Die lustige Witwe" — Franz Lehár
12. Marsch "Kaiser Brigade" — Blankenburg

Graphische Werkstätte Camp 3

A choir and orchestra concert held in March 1917 in camp III, compound 2.

Camp 3 — Comp. 2

KNOCKALOE, Isle-of-Man.   10. u. 21. MÄRZ 1917.

GROSSES CHOR und ORCHESTER KONZERT

Dirigent: Herr Hutmacher.

1. Ouverture "IL GUARANY" (A. Gomes) — Orchester
2. "WALDEINSAMKEIT" (J. Pache) — Chor
3. Fantasie aus "FAUST" (Gounod) — Orchester
4. "VALE CARISSIMA" (Thomass) — Chor
5. Fantasie aus "TOSCA" (Puccini) — Orchester
6. Bariton-Gesänge: Herr Carlo Martinolich
   a) "Am Meer" (F. Schubert)
   b) "Triste Ritorno" (R. Barthélemy)
   Am Klavier: Herr Hutmacher.
7. "LIEDESWEIHE" (M. v. Weinzierl) — Chor & Orchester

PAUSE

8. Walzer: "SIRENENZAUBER" (Waldteufel) — Orchester
9. "TRINKERLIED" (A. Reiser) — Chor
10. Herr WAGSCHAL
    Am Klavier: Herr Finkelstein.
11. Potpourri: "NA, DENN MAN LOS" — Orchester
12. "SÄNGERMARSCH" (V. E. Becker/Urbach) — Chor
13. "SIEGESMARSCH" (Ganne) — Orchester

ANFANG 6:30.

100 YEARS OF HISTORY 75

Redaktions Exemplar

Juli 1917.   Preis 2 d.

Zivilgefangenen-Halbmonatsschrift

DOH

CAMP-LITERATUR

:: ::   INHALT: :: ::

Gedicht.
Verlust der deutschen Staatsangehoerigkeit durch Abwesenheit.   H. W.
Spaniens Stellung im gegenwärtigen Weltkriege.   Funke.
Geschichtliche Gedenktafel.
Die Weltesche.   H. W.
Glaube u. Gegenwart.   Pastor Hartmann.
Süd-Amerika.   Dr. W. Kundt.
Was ist die Lage der Hotel-Angestellten nach dem Kriege.
:: :: CAMP-NACHRICHTEN :: ::
:: Schule. -- Sport. -- Theater. ::

Nr. 4.

Herausgegeben, Druck und Verlag:
R. M. CONRAD KIRCHNER, CAMP-DRUCKEREI
CAMP I   ::   COMPOUND IV
Knockaloe, Isle of Man.

Opposite: A choir and orchestra concert held in March 1917 in camp III, compound 2.

Left: The camp also had a bi-monthly literature magazine edited, printed and published by Herr Conrad Kirchner at the camp's printing facility in camp I compound IV. The magazine published stories and articles by the inmates and featured a news section covering education, sports and entertainment.

A commemorative art card which mentions staying faithful to old Germany.

100 YEARS OF HISTORY

1917
WEIHNACHT

DURCH DIE KALTEN WINTERLÜFTE
NAHT EIN WOHLBEKANNTER KLANG,
IN DER TANNE WÜRZ'GE DÜFTE
MISCHT SICH TRAUTER WEIHNACHTSANG.

KNOCKALOE. I. o. M.

Good draughtsmanship and simple elegant design in this printed three colour Christmas card for 1917. The text tells us that through the cold draughts of winter, a well known sound nears; familiar Christmas songs intermingle with the strong smell of the fir trees.

With a heavenly choir at the top and a stylised view of home in the panel underneath as imagined by the inmates of the more realistically illustrated camp and surroundings, this card commemorates the Christmas and the New Year for 1916-17:

Tree of homeland-faithfulness crowned by the star of the wise men brings endless charm in this valley of the Island.

An army of choirs sing thanks to the wrestling of the heroes, thanks to the sacrifices of love which are without number.

For you the happiness of Christmas, even better after agony, you should see the homeland in the new year!

Our thoughts are happily entwined around greeting our loved ones and the whole troop of friends.

Faithful greetings from Knockaloe.

100 YEARS OF HISTORY   79

This colour calendar dated 1918 features the four seasons illustrated in each corner panel using views of the camp. The upper middle panel appears to symbolize some of the craft and educational activities carried out by inmates with books, an artist's pallette and brushes, a wood plane and a model ship shown amongst other items. The lower middle panel advertises the printing facility within the camp responsible for the production of this fine piece of colour lithographic work with both the printer and the artist named.

KNOCKALOE INTERNMENT CAMP

Herzlichste Neujahrswünsche aus Knockaloe Camp, I. o. M.

New Year art card for 1917-1918 by Emil Reichet. The use of Manx symbology on printed items was taken for granted by this time.

100 YEARS OF HISTORY   81

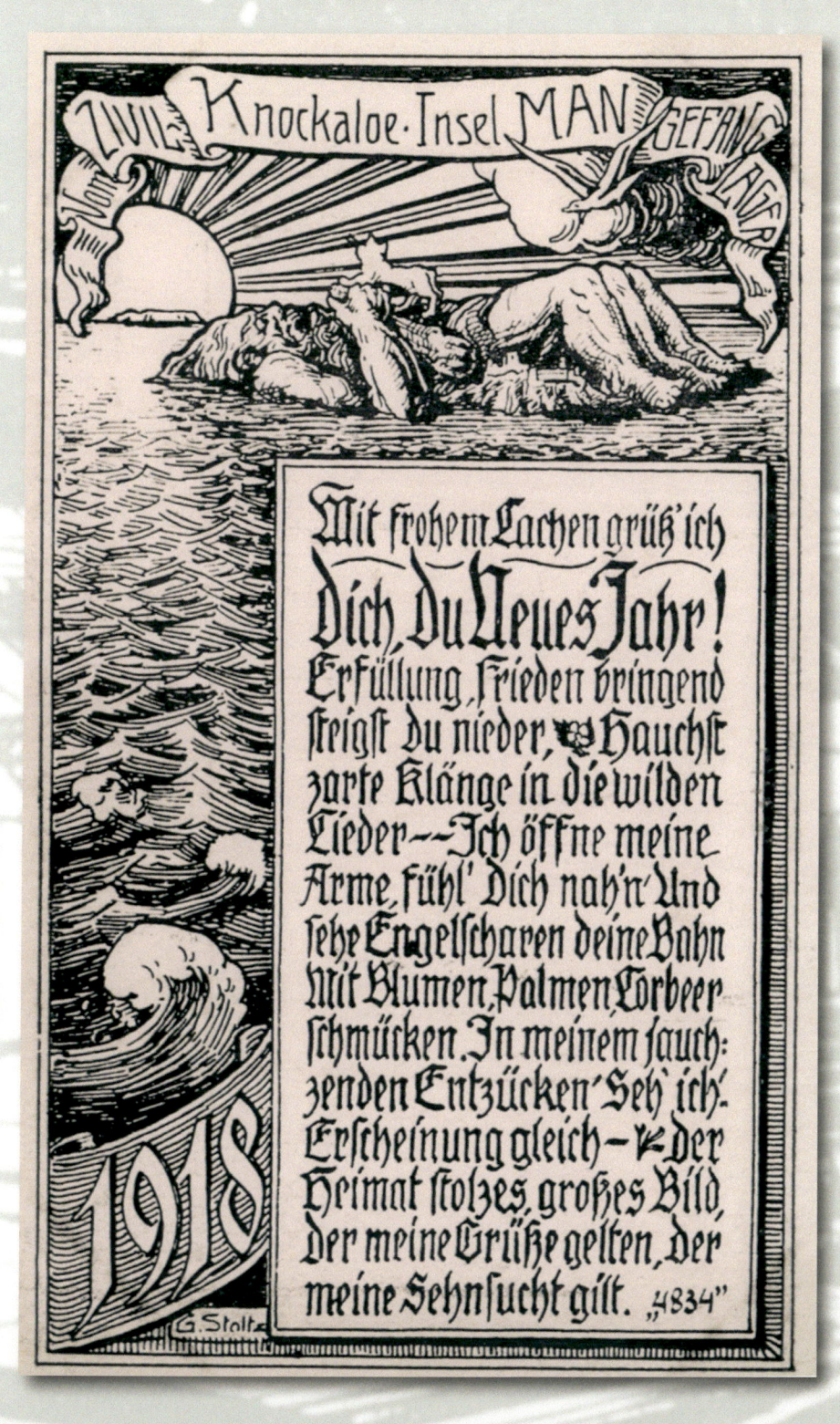

Another excellent New Year art card by G. Stoltz. Perhaps the giant lying in the sea represents Manannan symbolising the Isle of Man? The dove of peace makes an easter appearance and the stylised sea and sunset are very well rendered.

KNOCKALOE INTERNMENT CAMP

Above and right: Front and back of a Knockaloe pass to allow a hairdresser into the camp.

Opposite: Twice yearly camp newspaper, The Camp Echo, for March 1918. The top piece headed Fastnacht (Shrove-tide – the bginning of Lent) features a poem while the main text underneath headed Betrachtungen (Considerations) questions why the inmates are still being held at Knockaloe after so many years.

2. Jahrgang.   KNOCKALOE-LAGER,   1. Maerz 1918.

Preis 1 Penny   This Paper has been submitted to the Censor.

Lager - Echo.

Zeitschrift fuer das Zivilgefangenen = Lager Knockaloe, Isle of Man.

Schriftleitung: Max Horner, III/5.

Inseratenpreis f.d. 1/32 Seite 1s.   **No. 2**   Anschrift: Lagerecho, Camp 3, Compound 5, Knockaloe, I.O.M.

Fastnacht 1918.

Pierrot und Pierrette
druecken sich in dunkle Ecken,
muessen sich mit ihrem Lachen
vor dem Ernst der Zeit verstecken.
Pfropfenknall, Confettischlachten,
Domino und seidne Fetzen,
wo seid alle ihr geblieben
wisst die Zeit wohl nicht zu schaetzen?

Oder habt auch ihr gesehen,
dass es nicht der Maske braucht,
dass so manches ohne Fastnacht
schon vor Narrheit foermlich raucht?
Kommt zu uns, die wir da schmachten,
Jahre schon, 'ne Ewigkeit;
kommt und fragt, wie wir uns fragen,
ob das nicht zum Himmel schreit.

Seht ihr, wie sie alle tanzen,
bunt, in seid'nem Flitterkram,
wie sie tollen, schreien, jauchzen
um das gold'ne Opferlamm?
Pierrot und Pierrette,
troestet euch, denn alles schwankt;
eure Narrheit muss verstummen,
wo so viel am Irrsinn krankt.

Betrachtungen.

Wir sitzen noch immer! Wenn diese Zeilen in Druck erscheinen, sind schon wieder sieben bis acht Wochen des neuen Jahres verstrichen. Und es ist immer noch die alte Leier. Trotz der immer schlimmer werdenden Vergesslichkeit und trotz des fast chronischen Gedaechtnisschwundes haben wir uns schon an die neue Endziffer in der Jahresangabe gewoehnt. Ein glatter, schoener Achter entfliesst der Feder, die dann ob dieser Anstrengung sofort erschoepft stille steht, weil — die Gedanken zum Fortsetzen mangeln. Auch hinterm Stacheldraht kann man sich nicht ganz dem Nimbus entziehen, den so ein Jahreswechsel mit sich bringt. Die Feste feiert man eben im Herzen, und unser Herz war es zu lange gewoehnt, dieses Fest zu begehen. Und nun? Nun ist auch diese neue vierte Ziffer schon wieder etwas Altes, in das man sich festgewurzelt hat. Wenn man aber beim nochmaligen Durchlesen seiner Schweiss kostenden Schriftdenkmaeler mit einem etwas misstrauischen Blicke das Datum streift, da bleibt man unwillkuerlich an der 8 haengen. Die Phantasie beginnt zu spielen, die in Flitterkram strahlende Schwester der Hoffnung. Sieht das Ding nicht aus wie zwei Kettenglieder, die eng aneinander geschweisst sind? Ist es nicht eine Schleife ohne Anfang und ohne Ende? Spielt diese ominoese 8 nicht die Rolle des mystischen Zeichens der Pythagoreer, des Pentagramms oder Drudenfusses, ist das Symbol unseres Kerkerdaseins? Fuehlen wir nicht um die Knoechel unserer Fuesse en Druck zweier zusammengeschmiedeter Kettenringe, die uns den Fleck bannen gleich den eisernen Kugeln der Schwerverbrecher? Sind wir nicht gleich diesen zu einer Sache, zu einer Nummer geworden, ueber die man verfuegt, ohne auf das noch pulsende Innenleben auch nur die geringste Ruecksicht zu nehmen? Ist unser Vegetieren hinter den rostigen Zacken des Drahtes nicht wie eine Schleife ohne Anfang, ohne Ende, ohne Sinn und ohne Zweck? Fast koennten wir stolz werden auf den Wert, der doch unbedingt in uns ruhen muss, da man sich so hartnaeckig ueber uns unterhaelt und — haelt. Und nach der Zeitspanne, die wir bereits, fern der Welt, in der Gefangenschaft gebuesst haben, wuerden wir uns kaum noch wundern, wenn diese augenblicklich noch aufrecht stehende 8, die unser Leben so nett versinnbildlicht, sich allmaehlich in die Wagerechte neigte und zu dem mathematischen Begriff der Unendlichkeit wuerde. Es kommt uns fast so vor, als ob die, in deren Macht es gegeben ist, uns wieder zu Menschen zu machen, in dem Kriegsgetuemmel ganz vergessen haetten, wie diese Schleife geloest werden kann. Ein Alexander der Grosse, der kurzer Hand den gordischen Knoten mit dem Schwerte zerschlaegt, ist leider noch immer nicht aufgestanden. Und wir wuerden aufblicken zu ihm wie zu einem zweiten Messias, zu unserem Retter vom Untergang. Zu einem derartigen abgekuerzten Verfahren gehoert allerdings ein ganzer Mann, der sich trotz der Freiheit, in der er selbst lebt, vorstellen kann, was es heisst, vier endlose Jahre in Gefangenschaft zu darben. Und diesen gibt es offenbar nicht! Quod licet Jovi, non licet bovi! Die babylonische Gefangenschaft, die nur achtundvierzig Jahre dauerte, scheint ihre Wiedergeburt zu erleben.

1914 nahm man uns die Freiheit. Mit gefesselten Gliedern erduldeten wir die Jahre 1915, 1916, 1917. Jetzt hat das Jahr mit der 8 am Ende uns erreicht. 1914, 1915, 1916, 1917, 1918! Wenn man diese progressive Reihe sieht, fasst einen das Grausen. "Humanitaet" heisst das Schlagwort unserer Zeit. Bittere Ironie! Uns duenkt sie ausgewandert! Oder aber, sie ist auf einem anderen Gebiete so stark in Anspruch genommen, dass sie keine Zeit hat, sich um uns zu kuemmern. Vielleicht ist ihr Fernbleiben auch darauf zurueckzufuehren, dass wir gegen das heilige, ungeschriebene internationale Recht verstiessen, indem wir hinter Stacheldraht kamen. Die Humanitaet arbeitet aber selbstverstaendlich nur in der legitimen Sphaere, wo man das Gesetz beachtet und noch haelt, wo man verwendet werden kann. Wenn sie uns mit Verachtung straft, wird es wohl unsere eigene Schuld sein. Wir haben ja auch noch einige Haare auf den Koepfen, die noch nicht gekruemmt sind.

Auch haben wir einen nicht wieder gut zu machenden Mangel aufzuweisen. Wir sind naemlich keine Reserveoffiziere, Und das raecht sich schwer. Haetten wir alle jenen Grad erreicht oder ergehen koennen, dann koennten wir jetzt im Gelobten Lande der Kriegsgefangenen den weiteren Verlauf des Weltdramas in Musse abwarten. Sie sind zwar trotz ihres Ranges auch nur Zivilisten, die ebenso wie wir in Feindesland oder auf neutralen Schiffen gefangen gesetzt wurden, mit dem Kriege also ebensowenig zu tun haben wie wir, doch wir goennen es ihnen, ja wir besitzen sogar eine solche Portion Altruismus, dass wir uns wegen der multi sequentes freuen. Nach dem Haager Abkommen sollten — soweit ins bekannt ist — nur jene Offiziere und Unteroffiziere ausgetauscht werden, die aktiven Anteil am Kriege genommen und bereits ueber achtzehn Monate gefangen waren. Dieses Prinzip ist nun durchbrochen worden, indem auch Zivilisten nach Holland kamen, die weder fuenfundvierzig Jahre alt noch krank sind, — soweit bei uns ueberhaupt noch von Gesundheit gesprochen werden kann — vor uns Zurueckgesetzten also nichts voraus haben. Und was dem einen recht ist, ist dem anderen billig.

Wir moechten an dieser Stelle nochmals auf das beruehmte Haager Abkommen zurueckgreifen. Von der Wirkung haben wir bisher nur wenig gespuert, aber wir verraten wohl kein Geheimnis, wenn wir behaupten, dass man sich mit dem Schicksal der Kriegsgefangenen beschaeftigte. Einige Glueckliche haben ja doch das grosse Los gezogen. Fortuna verteilt diese Lose. Doch moechten wir uns die Frage erlauben, warum man uns, die wir doch sozusagen mitbeteiligt sind, im Finstern tappen laesst, bis wir muehsam aus verzerrten Zeitungsberichten, aus entsprechend abgefassten Weissbuechern, aus den mageren Mitteilungen von offizieller Seite, deren jede einzelne zu sensationsluesternen Affichen benuetzt wird, eine schwache Ahnung von dem Resultat zusammenstoppeln?

Man sollte diese Gelegenheit wirklich nicht vorruebergehen lassen. Die Wuerfel sind nun doch gefallen. Vielleicht koennten auch wir den Rubikon ueberschreiten. Schliesslich war ja doch die Frage der Tonnage die wichtigste. Alle anderen Ammenmaerchen glauben wir nicht. Wir paar Maennecken werden ja das Zuenglein an der Wage doch nicht mehr beeinflussen.

Stundenplan.

Zeit	Montag	Dienstag	Mittwoch	Donnerstag	Freitag	Sonnabend	Sonntag
9 bis 10	4. Engl. IV 5. Franz. II Spanisch	4. Engl. I 5. Tuerk. II Franzoes.	1. Botanik 4. Esperanto 5. Ital. I 8. Engl. II Kauf. Rechn.	4. Engl. IV 5. Franz. II Spanisch	4. Engl. I 5. Tuerk. II Franzoes.	3. Botanik 4. Esperanto 1. Ital. I 8. Engl. II Portugies. Rechnen	
10.15 bis 11	1. Deutsch 4. Fz. III 5. Fz. I Englisch	1. Deutsch 5. Span. II 6. Zeichnen Schiffahrt	1. Franz. IV 3. Deb.-Sch. 4. Ital. II 5. Franz. I Italien. Tuerkisch	1. Engl. III 4. Franz. III. 5. Span. II 6. Zeichnen Englisch Russisch	1. Deutsch 5. Franz. I Bergbau usw.	1. Franz. IV 3. Deb.-Schr. 4. Ital. II 5. Span. II 6. Zeichnen Italienisch Tuerkisch	Turnen
11 bis 11.45	1. Stolze-Sch. 4. Russisch Geschichte	4. Algebra A 5. Daenisch 6. Zeichnen Volkswirtsch.	1. Stolze-Schr. Rechtslehre	6. Zeichnen Geschichte	1. Stolze-Schr. 4. Russisch 5. Daenisch Volkswirtsch.	3. Algebra A 6. Zeichnen Rechtslehre	Turnen
11.45 bis 12.30	Geographie	5. Algebra 6. Zeichnen Bes. Geb. d. Volkswirtsch.	Buchfuehr.	6. Zeichnen Geographie	Bes. Geb d. Volkswirtsch.	5. Algebra 6. Zeichnen Buchfuehr.	Turnen
2 - 3	Musik-Probe	7. Elektrotech. 4. Spanisch I	1. Zahnarzt Musik-Probe	7. Elektrotech. 4. Span. I	Musik-Probe	3. Zahnarzt 4. Span. I 7. Elektrotech.	Schach-K
3 - 4		1. Sp. Vortr. 7. Elektrotech.		7. Elektrotech. 1. Sp. Vortr.		1. Span. Vrtr. 7. Elektrotech.	"
4 - 5							"
6 - 7	Theater-Probe	Vorlesungen Landwirtsch. T.V.	Theater-Probe	Vorlesung Landwirtsch. T.V.	Theater-Probe.	Vorlesungen Landwirtsch. T.V.	T.V.
7 - 8		Gesang		Gesang		Gesang	
8-9.45		Turnen		Turnen		Turnen	

Above and opposite: A timetable for the half year from winter 1918. The range of language classes on offer must reflect the various nationalities who were detained at Knockaloe. Even Esperanto, designed to be a common language across the world, was being offered. The front of the timetable celebrates the achievments of industry.

100 YEARS OF HISTORY

Schiffsingenieur-Unterklasse : Alle Wochentage von 9 - 1 und 2 - 4.

Abiturientenklasse : Alle Wochentage von 9 - 1 und 6 - 7.

Die Ziffern vor den Unterrichts-Stunden weisen auf die Schulplaetze hin.

Die Kurse oberhalb der punktierten Linien stehen im Rahmen der Schulkurse, die unterhalb der punkt. Linien im Rahmen der Handelswissenschaftlichen Kurse.

Lehrplan
der
Lagerschule
Knockaloe, Lager 3 Teillager 5
für das
Winter-halbjahr
1918/19
Schul--Leitung:
Joh. Rentzel — Kurt Blumenau

Liste der Verstorbenen.

Name	Alter	Camp
Hartmann, Frank	26	1
Raute, Hans Erdmann	19	1
Kasper, Michael	30	2
Kupfer, Peter	26	1
Büschking, Friedrich	19	1
Lembke, Ludwig Friedrich	49	2
Hoffmann, Heinrich	59	2
Meerwald, Ernst	32	3
Magura, Vasili	21	1
Steller, Julius	40	2
Bönnemann, Theodor	31	4
Fürth, Hans August Karl	26	1
Arendt, Rudolf	39	1
Schale, Wilhelm	57	3
Fuchs, Leonhardt	44	2
Winter, Herrmann	21	1
Wolber, Matthias	41	2
Wezel, August	52	2
Sawka, Stephan	47	2
Geislinger, Georg Michael	63	2
Ratzenberger, Hans	21	3
Klöker, Max Karl Ludwig	22	1
Molitor, Ferdinand	33	2
(Seefeld) Siefels, Wilhelm	54	3
Trömmer, Alexander Charles	61	1
Baackh, Georg	39	1
Becker, Friedr. Heinr. Christian	53	1
Rösch, Anton	44	1
Schütz, Johann Friedrich	60	1
Matzke, Gustav	46	4
Bierkamp, Albert	44	4
Conrad, Richard Walter	40	1

Liste der Verstorbenen: List of the deceased. This list shows the names and ages of those who passed away during internment.

100 YEARS OF HISTORY   87

THE BURIAL
GROUND PATRICK
I.O.M.

New graves at Patrick church and graveyard. The internees raised money themselves for the upkeep of these graves.

KNOCKALOE INTERNMENT CAMP

These two art cards show the hut layouts in the camp from a similar viewpoint with the hills in the background.

100 YEARS OF HISTORY   89

Above: Easter card for 1917.

Left: This detailed pen and ink drawing illustrates what the interior of one of the large huts would have looked like. With so many people crowded into a relatively small space it would have been difficult to retain any privacy. The latin inscription 'Pro Patria' means 'For Homeland'.

Above: This superbly atmospheric watercolour painting by Fritz Zimmermann produced in 1915 gives a great impression of camp life inside a hut with washing hanging from the rafters.

Opposite: Certificate awarded in a chess competition. This was printed on the Camp III's own litho press on New Year's Day 1919. Stephen particularly loves this item because of the dragon around the top of the design holding a shield with the three legs of man.

100 YEARS OF HISTORY

Ehren-Urkunde

womit beglaubigt wird, daß

Herr Karl Gwirtner

bei dem Inter Camp Turnier Knockaloe im Sommer 1918 den III. Preis errungen hat.

Für den Ausschuß

Ernst Carl Meyer   A. C. Reindl...

LITHOPRESSE DES UNTERRICHTSWESENS CAMP I. 1.1.19.

KNOCKALOE INTERNMENT CAMP

Knockaloe's Camp, Peel, Isle of Man

Above: Colour art card showing simplified design treatment with clean straight lines and blocks of colour.

Opposite: Another of Stephen's favourite art cards, showing members of the band practising under the moon on a fresh night. Note the snow on the rooftop and Corrins Tower top left.

100 YEARS OF HISTORY   93

WEIHNACHTS GRÜSSE
UND   PROSIT NEUJAHR
KNOCKALOE ISLE OF MAN · CAMP IV COMP 4
C. Stiehl   Nº 18871

KNOCKALOE INTERNMENT CAMP

> Häschen in der Heimat
> Sieht ein seltsam Bild.
> „Häschen! S'ist ein
>   Gruss von mir,
> Der auch einmal wild
> Heimatwald
>   durchstreifte.
> Seit ich ferne bin,
> Manches Gute reifte
> Mir im ernsten Sinn.
> Denke Dein um
>   Weihnacht!
> Wäre gern daheim.
> Mög's bescheren,
>   Dir und mir,
> Was ich glücklich
>   träum'!"
>
> GSt.

KNOCKALOE-CAMP, I.O.M.

A Christmas card with a poem. The author writes as someone who went through the woods back home, and sends a greeting to the rabbit depicted. Since he's far away his sober-mindedness has increased as has his maturity, good things have come of serious thinking. He tells the reader to think about themselves and their wishes at Christmas, he would like to be at home, and writes that may what we wish for happen, those things we dream about.

HERZLICHE OSTER-GRÜSSE
A.D. KNOCKALOE-CAMP

HOFFNUNG

Und dräut der Winter noch so sehr
Mit trotzigen Gebärden,
Und streut er Eis und Schnee umher,
Es muss doch Frühling werden.

Und wenn dir oft auch bangt u. graut,
Als sei die Höll' auf Erden,
Nur unverzagt auf Gott vertraut!
Es muss doch Frühling werden.

Geibel

This is another fine example of a commemorative Easter card. The inscription at the top offers Kind easter Greetings while the poem below promises that spring is on its way despite the ice and snow.

Poster advertising an exhibition of arts and craft work produced in 'the English prisoner of war camp' between 4-10 October 1915 with a Manx cat shown on the windowsill. Again the camp huts can be seen outside the window with Corrins Tower on the hillside in the distance. Another fine illustration by G Stoltz.